YOUTH SUICIDE

Depression and Loneliness

YOUTH SUICIDE
Depression and Loneliness

Brent Q. Hafen, Ph.D. and Kathryn J. Frandsen

CORDILLERA PRESS, INC.
Publishers in the Rockies

Library of Congress Cataloging-in-Publication Data

Hafen, Brent Q.
   Youth suicide.

   Bibliography: p.
   Includes index.
   1. Youth—United States—Suicidal behavior.
2. Adolescent psychology—United States.   I. Frandsen, Kathryn J.   II. Title.
HV6546.H345   1986·   362.2   86-19665
ISBN 0-917895-11-8

Second Edition
1 2 3 4 5 6 7 8 9

ISBN: 0-917895-11-8

Printed in the United States of America

Contents

Introduction

Gail was an energetic, talented sixteen-year-old who won friends easily and got involved in a wide range of activities at school. She played the flute in the school band and had been in several school plays, once in the leading role. She had developed a flair for oration and had won several small trophies for competition in multi-school debate meets. When junior varsity cheerleading tryouts were announced, no one was surprised when Gail scratched her name hastily across the tryout sheet — she was a natural!

More than three dozen of the most popular sophomore girls added their names to the lined sheet in the week it was posted in the girls' gym, and Gail found herself lingering nervously for a minute or two each day to see if any new names had been listed. She wanted more than anything to be a cheerleader, and this was the first step: you almost never became a cheerleader without first being accepted as a member of the junior varsity squad.

At the end of the week, a new notice was posted above the lined tryout sheet with its three dozen names: four practice sessions would be held after school in the next two weeks so that each girl could learn the routines and get into shape. At the end of the two-week period, tryouts would be held before the entire sophomore class, assembled on the shaky bleachers at the edges of the football field. The group of five cheerleaders would be chosen by a small group of faculty advisors and by popular vote of the sophomore class.

Gail was outfitted in her tights and ready on the polished wooden floor of the gym ten minutes early the afternoon of the first practice session; as she did slow stretching exercises to warm up, three of her closest friends sat, their backs against the wall, chattering animatedly. They were there for "moral support," even though they were sure Gail would make it. As Gail went through her stretching routine, she, too, was sure that she could conquer this, just as she had conquered everything else she had tried for.

A few minutes later, Gail wasn't so sure anymore. The routine was difficult and complex, and she had a hard time remembering what came next. It was hard work, too. The beads of perspiration that peppered her forehead became rivulets of salty sweat that stung her eyes; her hair clung to the back of her neck, and she felt the stabbing pain of a cramp in the arch of her foot. At last the advisor called for a break, and Gail sunk to the floor in a heap, breathing with deep, irregular gasps. She tried to look around at the other girls nonchalantly. They didn't seem to be nearly as winded or wiped out as she was; several of them sat in a small circle, laughing about the routine as though it were nothing.

The second half of the practice session was tougher than the first. Gail somehow fumbled through it, once or twice making wrong moves, and once, near the end, tripping into another girl. Her friends, leaning against the gym wall, tittered and snickered with careless abandon — she'd catch on!

As they walked home along the weed-choked sidewalk, Gail was much more quiet than usual; her three friends recounted the practice session, commenting on Gail's hilarious fumbles and another girl's outrageous leotard. Gail gazed intently at the crumbling concrete and felt her face flushing as she remembered her extreme effort at getting the routines right. It was so hard, and she hadn't expected it to be hard! She knew she would never make it. Most of the others had swept across the gym floor with grace and ease, inviting the advisor's approving nods; Gail had stumbled clumsily, her movements stiff and awkward. The music from the speakers filled her with a confusing roar, and she couldn't seem to pick out the simple beat so crucial to the routine. Her heart pounded against her chest, and her mouth felt as though it were full of cotton. Remembering it filled her with dread and embarrassment. The next rehearsal was Thursday afternoon; she had a long way to go before then.

The next morning, Gail's mother moved quickly down the hall, retrieving each of her three children from the night's heavy sleep. There was only half an hour until the bright yellow school bus rattled up to the curb, and she herself had overslept. She flung Gail's door open and shouted a cheerful greeting, but Gail didn't move. She was dead, an empty prescription sleeping pill bottle shoved under her pillow.

*   *   *   *

Kirk's family had settled into their suburban New York home late in March, just as the weather along the eastern seaboard had begun to warm and the delicate crocus had pushed their way through the still-frozen soil at the edge of the flowerbed. It had been a stark contrast to the Iowa farm where Kirk had grown up. During those first few months, he had spread across his bed, staring at the ceiling and remembering the splintering wood of the old barn, the endless cornfields with their yellowed stubble, the gentle milk cow tethered to the fence where he stood at dawn to catch a ride to school.

Settled in his cramped neighborhood, where the houses pressed against each other and the asphalt stretched forever, Kirk remembered the wide, rolling hills surrounding the frame farmhouse and the gravel road that snaked toward the house from the corner where the mailbox stood. He remembered waking before dawn, going with his friends to a tranquil pool along the river where they cast homemade fishing lines into the cool, clear water. They would kick off their dusty shoes and dangle their feet into the edge, even though they knew it would scare any fish away. Kirk missed those guys — missed the times when he could tell them the deepest secrets buried in his heart. There was no one like that in New York; Kirk had tried to make friends those first few weeks, but he felt brushed aside. He was the "farmer," the odd man out, the guy who was worn around the edges, thrown in among the sophisticated city kids.

At last he found a soulmate. Ron had grown up in New York, but not in the crowded confines of the concrete city; instead, he had spent his boyhood on a rambling farm in western New York. The hollyback had twined along the fence surrounding his two-story house, and a profusion of morning glory had bloomed at the edges of the pasture. Ron told Kirk all about his milk cow and his small herd of goats, and of the time he and a friend had won a prize at the state fair.

The two were inseparable for the rest of the school year, and as the sticky humidity of the New York summer slowed most of the neighborhood into a lethargic hum, Ron and Kirk munched pizza under the umbrella at a sidewalk cafe and rode the bus or the subway to the outer limits of the sprawling city. Kirk found that he could at last be himself — that he could stop trying to hide the face that he would rather be splashing in the pond along the stream than dashing in and out of the sprinklers on the front lawn.

In the middle of August, just as ne was starting to think about school and just as the heat became the most oppressive, Kirk found out that Ron's family was moving to Nebraska. His father had accepted a position at a university there and steered the large U-Haul truck up over the lawn until it rested against the front porch. The house belched forth its goods, and most of the family crowded into the green Chevrolet that followed behind. Kirk stood in the heat along the curb and waved until the last hint of taillights disappeared around the corner at Madison Drive. His bicycle seat dug into his thigh as he pedaled toward his own frame house, squeezed into the crowded subdivision. His friend was gone, and he couldn't face the prospect of trying to find another one.

Digging through his bottom drawer, he found the thick leather belt he had worn so often with his faded Levis. He looped one end around the closet rod, the other around his neck. With a snap, his despair was over.

*   *   *   *

News of Karin's suicide rocked the quiet community in

eastern Montana. She had been the epitome of teenage success and happiness — a pretty, popular, talented girl, she had been crowned the school's homecoming queen the year before. At the age of seventeen, she had positioned her father's handgun against her forehead and had pulled the trigger in an act of desperation and rage that no one understood.

No one except Hal, that is — Hal, who had been with Karin earlier that night. As hundreds of mourners filed past her flower-bedecked coffin and whispered their strained condolences to her numbed parents, Hal remembered Karin the way she had been that night. He had gotten panicked, worried about his gradually dying independence and freedom; he had imagined Karin was hemming him in, pressing him for a commitment that he wasn't ready to make. He had told her it was over — had pushed her out of the front seat of his car as he sat in her driveway, had ignored her pleas to reconsider. Hal sat in the corner of the funeral home in an overstuffed chair that almost swallowed him; he stared at the coffin and heard Karin's last words pounding through his head. In half an hour, the funeral would begin. In an hour, after sad music and tearful words at the pulpit, the procession would wind its way to the city cemetery, and Karin's body would be lowered into the cooling ground. In a month, the October frost would lace the soil, and the first of winter's bitter blizzards would whip across the frozen wheatfields.

The chapel was packed for the funeral, and only a few people noticed that Hal wasn't there. Dozens of Karin's friends huddled around the gravesite, wishing her a final farewell. But Hal wasn't there, either. He had gone home, climbed the narrow stairs into the attic, and put a bullet through his forehead.

*   *   *   *

Clear Lake City, Texas, a community of 37,000 that houses the Johnson Space Center, is one of dozens of communities scattered across the country that has known the shock and despair of "cluster suicides," chains of deaths among teenagers that devastate the survivors. Clear Lake City's series of suicides began with Paul Kuns, a nineteen-year-old who shot himself in the head in his car. Two of his friends — high school dropouts like Paul — followed in rapid succession: Sean Woods, also nineteen, shot himself in the head in his pickup truck, and a few weeks later another nineteen-year-old member of the group, Wesley Tiedt, was found hanging from the top of a stairway in his home.

Clear Lake City's cluster suicides were not confined to Kuns and his circle of friends, however. Two days after Tiedt was found hanging, fifteen-year-old Lisa Schatz shot herself. Three days later, sixteen-year-old Gary Shivers was found hanging in his garage. Two days later, fourteen-year-old Darren Thibodeaux sealed off the family garage with bath towels, turned on the motor of the car, and died of carbon monoxide poisoning.

*   *   *   *

Farther north in the sun-baked state of Texas lies Plano, a Dallas suburb considered to be "the quintessential Sun Belt city," according to the *Los Angeles Times*, and a "perfect city," according to the *Texas Monthly*. Subject to a population explosion that began in the early 1970s and now known for its corporate achievers, Plano has been transformed from a stretch of lonely black-earth cotton farms into a grid of upper-middle-class subdivisions.

But everything in Plano is not perfect. Its divorce rate is one of the highest in the nation, and it is plagued by an overriding sense of boredom and restlessness. And it had been rocked by a series of cluster suicides among its young people.

The trouble apparently started with the death of seventeen-year-old William Ramsey, who was killed in a drag-racing accident. While Ramsey's death was not classified as a suicide, it did prompt the suicide of his best friend, a sixteen-year-old who was devastated by the loss. Two other suicides followed in rapid succession, and sixteen others between the ages of thirteen and twenty-four attempted suicide unsuccessfully. The methods used by the Plano teenagers were as varied as they themselves were: one girl carved up her chest with a pair of scissors, a boy tried to hang himself with his own shirt, another boy slashed himself with a razorblade, and some took overdoses of various medicines — including Anacin, Alka-Seltzer, Tylenol, Sominex, and Valium.

*   *   *   *

Peekskill, New York, is a usually peaceful kind of place. On most afternoons, kids gather in the town park to play a fast-paced game of touch football or to toss a frisbee in the drifting breeze. But in February 1984, a chain of events began that transformed the quiet community into a bedlam of shocked terror.

Robbie DeLaValliere was a well-liked seventh-grader at Peekskill Middle School; he had dozens of friends and no history of psychiatric problems of any kind. He was one of the regulars at the grassy park, pitching a tattered softball to anybody who'd pull a leather mitt on. He liked to watch television, frequently went to the movies with his friends, and did well at school. On February 4, Robbie had gone to the park, but he shuffled around the edges instead of joining in with the others. Sometime before dark he chose a sturdy tree, wrapped a length of rough-hewn rope around a stocky branch, and — without seeming cause — hung himself. He had recently seen the movie *An Officer and A Gentleman*, in which a young Navy cadet hangs himself; police speculated that Robbie's suicide may have been a form of imitation.

Justin Spoonhour lived in Peekskill, too, but he went to Putnam Valley Junior High School. He was different from Robbie in many other ways, too. Justin found it extremely difficult to make friends; he seemed to have more in common with the teachers at Putnam Valley than he did with his fellow seventh-graders. Rumpled and gangly, he was an extremely bright boy (with what school administrators estimate was a near-genius-level IQ) who liked to listen to Beethoven and Brahms more than he did Michael Jackson or Boy George. Justin had been meeting with the school psychologist, too — his parents had been concerned because Justin just wasn't "fitting in."

But just ten days after Robbie DeLaValliere hanged himself from a sturdy tree in the park, Justin Spoonhour wandered into the woods behind his family's house and hanged himself from a tree. It was Valentine's Day and his mother wondered if maybe Justin was dismayed over the prospect of "nobody to love."

Westchester County, which sprawls along the northern border of New York state, had not seen the last of the shattering suicides. Two days after Justin was found in the wooded hills behind his home, nineteen-year-old Sleepy Hollow High School senior James Pellechi shot himself through the head in his North Tarrytown home. The suicide seemed to be linked to dejection by a girlfriend: "If you don't go out with me tonight," he had told her sullenly, "you'll be sorry tomorrow." She heard the bang as the receiver hit the floor, and seconds later heard the crack of gunfire.

Five days later, Christopher Ruggiero — godson of the Pelham town mayor and seventeen-year-old son of Westchester County's fire chief — was found hanging by a bathrobe sash in his closet. A curly-haired junior at Pelham High School, he was talented and well-liked. He had been named the best player on his school's hockey team, and he got

---

"We are said to be in the midst of an epidemic of adolescent suicide. Every city and community, from the tidy row-house neighborhoods of the northeast corridor to the affluent new suburbs of the Sun Belt, has its horror story of the bright young student with the unlimited potential who brutalizes the sensitivities of his or her family and friends with this most wanton act of self-abuse. In an epidemic, the statistics become stupefying . . . But behind these statistics are the young people — sons and daughters, brothers and sisters, students and friends — who were not able to find a way out of their pain or confusion or loneliness. It is up to us to help those who have yet to face similar crises."

— *Herbert Pardes, M.D., Former Director, National Institute of Mental Health, in* Youth Suicide *(Michael Peck, Norman Farberow, and Robert Litman, Editors)*

along well with his parents. The reason behind his tragic suicide? He had been suspended from the hockey team after arguing with an official.

Before Christopher Ruggiero had been buried, nineteen-year-old Arnold Caputo hanged himself in the attic of his parents' stately $250,000 home in Westchester County. An accomplished guitarist, Arnold was described as a "happy, all-American guy" who seemed to have everything going for himself. He didn't take drugs, never drank alcohol except for an occasional beer, and was pulling straight A's at Fordham University. He had just formed a new band and had recently cut his first album. When he remarked to a friend the day before his suicide that he couldn't "take it any more," the friend thought he was merely disenchanted with the band. Apparently his drive for musical success had convinced him he was failing: he had been turned down on several bids to perform as the warmup band for some name groups. One of his friends summed up, "He wanted to establish himself at an early age. Maybe because he was turning twenty, he just freaked out."

Less than a month later, nineteen-year-old Brian Hart of Bedford — and son of Bedford's town clerk — killed himself in his own car by carbon monoxide poisoning. Brian, and the five before him, failed to leave suicide notes indicating what prompted their desire to die. Their deaths cast a feeling of despair and panic over their well-to-do parents, teachers, and friends, who felt helpless to stop the tide of killings.

Researchers know very little about cluster suicides. Some may be merely conicidences; others may be self-dramatizing efforts to capture the same outpouring of sympathy that surrounded an earlier death.

Dr. Mark Rosenberg of the Centers for Disease Control in Atlanta believes that clusters probably occur "much more frequently than we find out about." Suicides generally tend to be underreported

Incidence of Youth Suicide

Teenage suicide has become a critical national problem. The extent of that problem is boggling: a teenager attempts suicide every ninety seconds, and another succeeds every ninety minutes. But the extent of that problem is difficult to estimate because many suicides are confused as accidents and others are not reported as suicides in order to save the family from embarrassment. Recent estimates, however, are disturbing: some feel that as many as 7,000 teenagers each year commit suicide, while an additional 400,000 try unsuccessfully to end their own lives. One expert in the field, Los Angeles psychologist Dr. Michael Peck, estimates that a million children each year think at one time or another about suicide — something he calls "an epidemic of suicidal communication among young people."

Suicide is now the second leading cause of death among adolescents — second only to accidents, some of which may be suicides. California's Suicide Prevention and Crisis Center recently released statistics that reveal a tragic trend: in two short decades, the suicide rate among children ten to fourteen years of age more than doubled; among those fifteen to nineteen years of age, it tripled. An increasingly high percentage of those who commit suicide each year fall within the adolescent age group. Dr. Pamela Cantor, president-elect of the American Association of Suicidology, calls teen suicide "a worldwide event, but only in the United States is it an epidemic."

According to statistics released by the Division of Vital Statistics of the National Center for Health Statistics and the Bureau of the Census, suicide rates among teenage girls (aged fifteen to twenty-four) jumped 200 percent during the past twenty-five years. The rate for boys in the same age group is even higher: during the past twenty-five years, it leaped 300 percent. Teenage girls now constitute approximately 15 percent of all suicides committed each year; teenage boys constitute approximately 20 percent. The suicide rate of teenage boys in the United States now surpasses those of all other nations in the world — including Japan and Sweden, long identified with a suicide problem.

Of particular interest to many is the suicide rate among American Indian adolescents. On many reservations, the rate has increased 200 to 300 percent in the last two decades; in that same period, the number of suicide attempts among American Indian adolescents has skyrocketed by almost 1000 percent. What it means is this: ten times as many American Indian youths today are attempting suicide than in 1965.

Calvin J. Frederick of the National Institute of Mental Health mentions a number of factors that could be leading to the increase in American Indian suicide: among them are alcoholism, drug abuse, and self-destructive behaviors that result from factors such as the dissolution of traditional Indian lifestyles; menial jobs and low job skills; the migration toward large cities; and stress.

In a brochure published by the National American Indian Court Judges Association, reports state that although there has been a dramatic rise in the suicide rate of American Indian adolescents in recent years, the rate has remained low on those reservations where the tribes are more traditional in their daily living and where employment and educational opportunities within the tribal community enable youths to remain at home.

Suicide rates are high among Great Plains tribes, for instance, which were relocated often or far from their original living areas. Also cited is research indicating that 50 percent of the American Indian adolescent suicides had experienced two or more parental losses by divorce or desertion compared to 10 percent of the nonsuicides. More than 80 percent of the suicides had one or more arrests in the twelve months preceding the suicide, compared to about 25 percent of the comparison group.

Environmental factors that may lead to adolescent Indian suicide, the study says, include the erosion of tribal tradition; a lack of effective role models; alcoholic parents; unemployment; and academic failure.

Another group of great concern is that of young Black males. In a recent interview with the *Behavior Today Newsletter,* Dwight Miles, a social worker from Baltimore, suggests that "the suicide rate among Black males between the ages of fifteen and thirty-four is higher than that of any other group. The phenomenally high rate of unemployment (officially listed as over 40 percent for at-risk age groups) among Black males is linked to this rate. But even these figures are misleading, he said.

"Part of the reason suicides among Blacks are underrepresented, he says, is that coroners attribute many suicides to accidental causes, such as those caused by overdose or those that are alcohol-related.

"Another reason for this underrepresentation is that there is a strong taboo against suicide in the Black community. People get really angry when I present this topic. They don't want to deal with the reality of the genocidal situation we face when you also consider the high rate of Black homicide."

"Did you know last year an estimated 2,000,000 American youngsters attempted suicide? Unless they receive the help they need and want, many of them will repeat their attempts, and thousands will end their young lives."

—*Youth Suicide National Center*

Is suicide an international problem?

Yes, say researchers — and Dr. Norman L. Farberow, codirector of the Los Angeles Suicide Prevention Center, points out the differing but alarming trends in material that he presented at the recent National Conference on Youth Suicide. In contrasting United States rates with those of several European countries, Far Eastern countries, and Canada, Dr. Farberow uses the number of suicide deaths per 100,000 living population in each age group. He chose the countries that he did for the study, he says, because of adequate certification and reliable statistics — two factors not always present in the countries of Africa, Central America, and South America.

In the United States, the rate for the general population has shown a steady increase over the past two decades, with the rate for males jumping to 20.1 suicides per 100,000, an increase of 22 percent during the past twenty years. While the rate for females has increased at a rate two and one-half times slower than that of males, it has still shown a sizeable increase. The greatest increase in suicides in the United States has been among young males — a suicide rate that has jumped 132 percent since 1965.

Canada has shown similar trends as have been demonstrated in the United States, with an even more dramatic increase among young males — a suicide rate that leaped 219 percent during the past two decades. The sharpest increase in the Canadian suicide rate has been among the youngest age group:

"Many seriously depressed youngsters are suicidal, yet their suicidal thinking is rarely recognized. We just don't want to hear about it, perhaps because we might not know what to do about it. Among adolescents, suicidal behavior is so common that it has moved during the past decade from the fourth to the second leading cause of death."

—Dr. John F. McDermott, Jr., M.D., *Professor of Psychiatry, John A. Burns School of Medicine, University of Hawaii at Manoa, Honolulu*

a rate that tripled, from 5.7 to 17.4, in twenty years.

The suicide rates among European nations, says Dr. Farberow, differ markedly. The general suicide rate in England and Wales, for example, has decreased; even the suicide rate among youth has seen a slight decrease, from 4.5 to 4.3 over the past twenty years. Sweden, traditionally known for a high suicide rate, has seen the number of suicides consistently drop since the early 1970s.

In France, the suicide rate among the general population has remained the same over the past twenty years — but, in stark contrast, the rate among young males has almost doubled. In West Germany, the suicide rate is similar to that in the United States, but the rate has been consistently decreasing since the late 1970s.

In stark contrast is Austria, which has experienced the same increase in suicide rates as has the United States — but, surprisingly, the increase in suicides among teenagers did not begin to occur until much later than throughout the rest of the world (starting in 1973, according to Dr. Farberow). Austria bears an interesting paradox, too: while it is a nation characterized by strong, widespread religious influence (more than 95 percent of the population is Roman Catholic), it also has one of the highest suicide rates on the continent.

The other European leader in suicide rates is Finland, which started with abnormally high suicide rates and which has experienced the widest variation in suicide rates. Among the general population, the rate increased from 19.8 to 25.8

"Youth suicide strikes at every level of society. Those we have already lost through suicide include the best and brightest of their generations. It is a national problem which can only be solved through the combined efforts of individuals, organizations, and government."

—*Charlotte P. Ross, Co-Chairperson, National Committee for Youth Suicide Prevention*

between 1965 and 1976; it has stayed the same since. The suicide rate among males, which increased by 31 percent and then stayed the same since 1976, is at the phenomenal high of 42.3 per 100,000. The suicide rate among young males skyrocketed almost 300 percent in one decade, and peaked at 45.8 from a low of 14.7.

In the Far East, the two countries with reliable statistics show a slightly different trend than that in the United States. Japan, with a general suicide rate that peaked at 18.0 in 1979, has experienced slight fluctuations since then — but no real increase or decrease. In Australia, the rate among young males has increased with fluctuations; the rate for young women has remained the same. The general suicide rate in Australia has remained the same for men and has dipped among women.

In the United States, one of the most disturbing aspects of the rate of teenage suicide is its recent surge — an increase that the American Academy of Child Psychiatry calls "dramatic." One study conducted on a college campus revealed that 70 percent of those questioned said that they had considered suicide as a serious option at some time in their lives.

In some cases, the teenager's life appears to be perplexingly ideal; there may be little or no indication of trouble to concerned parents, friends, and teachers. Many come from close-knit, loving families, and have a history of success and popularity at school. Some suicidal adolescents seem calm and peaceful; others seem depressed, lonely, or unable to fit in. Only one thing links all suicidal teenagers: *each one believes that suicide is the*

"Youth suicide is a phenomenon which is at once perplexing, contradictory, frightening and troubling. It is so troubling that we avoid talking about it. As individuals and as a nation we do not want to believe that a young person just emerging from childhood can feel the degree of sadness and despair that leads to suicide."

—*Youth Suicide National Center*

only option.

Stemming the tide of teenage suicide will take understanding of suicide itself, insight into the struggles that mark normal adolescent development, and a clear indication of potential causes, warning signs, and prevention techniques.

In a recent article by Joseph Alper, the following startling comment about youth depression and suicide was made:

> "The chilling fact is that we may be on the verge of an epidemic-like increase of mania, depression and suicide," says Elliot S. Gershon, chief of the clinical psychogenetics branch at NIMH. "The trend is rising almost exponentially and shows no signs of letting up. I would go so far as to say this is going to be *the* public health problem of the 1990s and beyond if the trend continues."

Even more startling is the prediction by the National Center for Health Statistics that by the year 2000 there will be another increase of 94 percent in suicide rates for fifteen- to nineteen-year-olds and a 114 percent increase for twenty- to twenty-four-year-olds.

Not only are we seeing an alarming increase in youth depression and suicide, but also in a number of other mental health areas. The American Academy of Child Psychiatry and the National Council of Community Mental Health Centers recently called attention to the following statistics.

—There has been an estimated increase of 350 percent in the number of adolescents admitted to private psychiatric hospitals in the last five years.

—In the fifteen- to twenty-four-year range, the leading causes of death are accidents, homicides, and suicides — all of which have a strong correlation with drug and alcohol abuse. Mortality rates in thhis age group have risen significantly in the last twenty years.

—Ten to 20 percent of adolescents are problem drinkers, and the arrest rate for intoxication for those under eighteen has tripled during the past decade.

—Between 5,000 and 6,000 teenagers committed suicide in one recent year.

—As many as 12 million children under eighteen — or 20 percent of American youth — suffer from mental health problems. Of these, approximately three million have serious psychiatric disorders.

Some of the most prevalent mental health problems affecting teenagers today are depression, drug and alcohol abuse, and conduct disorders (persistently defying the rights of others, or violating age-appropriate norms). Teenage girls in particular suffer from anorexia nervosa (a refusal to eat leading to a weight loss of at least 25 percent) and bulimia (a compulsion to binge on large amounts of food and then purge by self-induced vomiting by the use of laxatives). Other mental illnesses that affect adolescents include learning disabilities, anxiety, schizophrenia, and attention deficit disorder (characterized by impulsivity, difficulty following directions, and often, hyperactivity).

Many of the factors discussed in the following pages may not only contribute to youth suicide but also to the above listed problems.

"Everything we know about suicide tells us that people who try to take their own lives really want desperately to find a better way. If there's a positive aspect to this, it's that the potential for prevention is very high. If the cry for help is not ignored, it can have a positive effect for bringing about change, for helping people turn desperate situations around and tapping their own strengths."

—Dr. J.E. Geist, Adolescent Psychiatrist, Milwaukee

Myths About Suicide

The first step toward a clear understanding of suicide is to identify and dismiss some of the popular myths. You've probably heard plenty of them and may even believe some of them. Some of the most common misconceptions include the following:

People who commit suicide always leave notes. None of the troubled teenagers in Westchester County left notes — and, in fact, only a small percentage of those who commit suicide leave notes explaining why or telling that they intentionally took their own life. This misconception is a particularly dangerous one — many suicides are labeled as "accidents" because friends, family members, and/or investigating officers did not find a suicide note.

People who commit suicide are psychotic or mentally ill. Some suicide victims are indeed psychotic; in fact, the risk of suicide increases if there is psychosis or mental illness. But many suicidal people are just severely depressed and can't figure out any other solution to their problems — they can't figure out any other way to make the pain stop. So don't think that a "normal" person is beyond self-destruction.

"Rich" people commit suicide more often than "poor" people

do. That's not true, either. Suicide is pretty evenly distributed among the socioeconomic groups.

People who talk about suicide are just trying to get attention; people who really commit suicide don't talk about it first. This is probably the most unfortunate misconception of all. Eight out of ten people who commit suicide give definite warning signs of their intentions; the other two usually give some kind of verbal clues. Almost no one commits suicide without first letting someone else know how he feels. A person who talks about committing suicide or who threatens to commit suicide is begging for help — he wants to be given an option so that he doesn't have to end his life. Listen! Pay attention! Never ignore a threat.

Suicide happens without warning. The clues may not always be verbal, but they are almost always there. People simply don't recognize them. Most suicidal people leave a host of clues and warnings about their intentions.

If someone has decided to commit suicide, there is nothing you can do to stop him. Sometimes that is true, but most of the time it's not. The majority of suicides can be stopped. Even a person who is severely depressed and seriously intent on suicide is probably torn between wanting to live and wanting to die — and you can push him toward the "living" side. Authorities have identified an ambivalence among suicidal people — they want to die, yet they want to live. A teenager

"In the last twenty years adolescents who have every advantage are becoming the high-risk suicide group. Oh, kids have always thought about it — feeling *suicidal is actually a common response for all of us when times get particularly difficult. But today more and more kids are* acting *on these thoughts — and succeeding."*

—*Dr. Kim Smith, Co-Director, The Menninger Suicide Research Project*

who jumped from the fourth story of an apartment building in an attempt to end his life was severely crushed in the fall but did not die immediately. As paramedics and onlookers rushed to his side, he frantically moaned, "Don't let me die! Don't let me die!"

For suicide to succeed, three things must happen: the person must want to die, the person must have the means to carry out his wish (a gun, for instance, or the knowledge and materials with which to hang himself), and the person must have energy enough to complete the act. Sometimes a person becomes so severely physically and mentally depressed that he can't carry out his own desire to kill himself — he simply doesn't have the energy.

A person who is once suicidal is suicidal forever. Most people who want to kill themselves are, in fact, suicidal for only a limited amount of time. Many can go on to lead normal lives once the suicidal crisis is worked through. The best prognosis occurs for people who only *think* about suicide but do not actually *attempt* it.

If a person attempts suicide but survives, he probably won't attempt it again. Here's where the difference lies between thinking about suicide and actually attempting it. The sad facts are these: four out of five people who succeed in committing suicide had made at least one previous attempt. People who try to commit suicide are very likely to try again; estimates say that about half of those who try will try again.

The secret lies in getting someone over the "hump"; if you can just pull someone out of a depression, he won't try to kill himself. Unfortunately, that's not always true. It can be baffling: most suicides occur within about three months of an apparent "improvement" in a severely depressed condition. Why? One reason was discussed above — a severely depressed person might not have the sheer energy to carry out his plans. Once he starts to "improve," he gets the energy he needs to follow through.

Amy's parents had been mildly concerned when she began to get despondent and depressed; she was normally such a cheerful, enthusiastic, energetic fifteen-year-old. Seemingly without warning her school work had started to suffer; she had lost interest in her usual activities, including the debate team, which she usually loved. She lost the spirit of competition, and didn't even want to do much with her friends. Her parents figured she was just going through a "phase," and were relieved when she started to pull out of it. One night she enthusiastically announced that she wanted to fix the family dinner. She carefully shaped a meatloaf, sliced the potatoes and carrots, and shredded a variety of vegetables into a crisp green salad. While the meatloaf finished cooking, she set the table with the best dishes and silverware, went upstairs to her room, put the barrel of a handgun in her mouth, and pulled the trigger.

Terminally ill people are the ones most likely to commit suicide. Knowledge of a terminal illness *can* lead to suicide in some cases — the person decides to take his own life rather than suffer the pain and disfigurement that comes along with a disease that will result in death anyway. Dr. Nathan Pritikin, author of the Pritikin diet designed to help coronary patients reduce their risk, took his own life when he discovered that the leukemia he had been battling was no longer in remission. But terminally ill people are not as likely to commit suicide as are chronically ill people — people who are tired of suffering and who see no cure or end to that suffering other than self-destruction. The tendency increases among those over the age of sixty.

"Youngsters who attempt suicide come from all classes of society and even include preschoolers. Among the shocking examples are a 6-year-old who tried to hang himself because he was a burden to his financially strapped family and a 14-year-old girl who knelt in front of a train after learning she was pregnant."

—U.S. *News & World Report*

Suicide is hereditary. Suicide does tend to "run in families," which has given the mistaken idea that it is (or can be) genetically inherited. Currently, it is believed that suicide is *not* a genetic trait. However, since members of families tend to share the same emotional climate and since coping can be a learned skill, suicide can be more common in some families than in others. The suicide of one family member tends to increase the risk among other family members — a person who is suffering from a deep depression sees that her mother ended her suffering through suicide, for example, and she does the same. She sees it as a "solution," as something that was "good enough for Mom." In some ways, her mother's suicide gives her "permission" to end her own life.

Some researchers are beginning to believe that suicide *may* have some genetic links, however; such research is in the infant stages, and there are no proven conclusions. In a presentation at the recent National Conference on Youth Suicide, Dr. Mark Rosenberg, M.D., Violence and Epidemiology Branch, Centers for Disease Control, shared the results of a series of studies on twins. Among seventy single-egg (or identical) twins, twins that shared the identical genetic makeup, there are thirteen twin pairs in which both twins committed suicide. Among 156 two-egg twins (twins that do not share the identical genetic makeup), there are *no* pairs in which both twins have committed suicide.

Still another study of the gentic link in suicide followed a number of children who had been adopted through the Denmark Adoption Registry. In cases where a biological parent committed suicide — even though the child did not know the

---

"Eleven-year-old Becky swallowed an entire bottle of aspirin. She said she did it because she didn't have anything to live for since she had just lost her best friend. After several months of erratic eating and sleeping, Becky tried again — this time she died.

—*Youth Suicide National Center*

biological parent or live with the biological parent — the child stood a much higher chance of committing suicide, even in the absence of depression or previous suicidal behavior.

Dr. Rosenberg, in commenting on the limited studies, points out the obvious flaw: the studies suggest that suicide may have some genetic link, but the studies do *not* tell us how suicide might be transmitted. Do children inherit a predisposition toward suicide? Do they inherit aggression, which they turn inward? No one knows — but Dr. Rosenberg feels that there is enough tantalizing information to justify seeking further evidence. Even he, though, admits that a genetic link in suicide is still sketchy.

The most common method of suicide is drug overdose. That's not true. The leading cause of death among suicide victims is gunshot wounds; those who take drugs are less often successful.

Most suicides happen late at night. That's not true, for a very simple reason — most suicidal people don't really want to die. The attempt at suicide is a plea for help in many cases, not an actual, intentional act of destruction. As a result, many suicides (and suicidal attempts) happen in late afternoon or early evening, when friends and family members are most likely to discover the victim and "save" him. A woman might overdose on sleeping pills at 4:30 p.m., for example, when she knows that

---

"Adolescents may not even know that there is a name for the way they are feeling. Few of them have found ways of dealing with depression and when these feelings overwhelm them, they frequently believe there is something very wrong with them. They need the help of adults and mental health professionals who care about them, and who possess the experience and coping skills they lack."

—Youth Suicide National Center

her husband will be home by 5:15 and will be able to intervene and save her (and, of course, he will immediately stop doing whatever it is that has driven her to this extreme). Only those who are truly intent on dying attempt suicide late at night, when sleeping friends and family members aren't going to be around to intervene.

You should never talk about suicide to someone who is depressed, because you'll give him ideas. Don't worry — those ideas probably already exist. If a person has not seriously considered suicide your talking about it won't plant those ideas in his head. On the contrary: the act of talking about suicidal ideas helps a person work through them. It helps him bring them to the surface, where he can confront them and work through them with directness and honesty. Someone who is dropping clues, however subtle, will be relieved to talk about it.

"Kids" don't commit suicide — especially kids under the age of fifteen. Unfortunately, that's not true: approximately 3 percent of those under the age of fifteen are suicidal, says Angela Gillis, assistant professor at St. Francis Xavier University. So don't shrug your shoulders and dismiss an apparent suicide threat just because you're dealing with a little child.

Everyone who commits suicide is depressed. Depression is a common factor leading to suicide, and many suicidal people are depressed — but depression is not always the cause (or even present). Some people simply wish to escape their life situation: fourteen-year-old Michelle was not necessarily depressed about being pregnant, but she knew that it would cause an uproar at home, would affect her relationships at school, and would probably wreck many things in her life. She needed to escape from that life situation and wasn't able to see any other options. She climbed into the family car late one night, drove it cautiously out onto the street, and slammed it into a concrete wall at high speed.

Other people are anxious or agitated. Some are psychotic. Some, as discussed, are in chronic pain and see no other way of getting relief from the pain.

People who commit suicide rarely seek medical help. Not true! Estimates say that half of those who commit suicide had sought medical help within the six months preceding the suicide.

Who Is At The Highest Risk?

What kind of a person is most likely to commit suicide? No one particular kind of person commits suicide. If there is one thing we have learned about suicide through considerable research, it is that suicide crosses all ages, races, cultures, sexes, and creeds with seeming little respect. But there *are* certain characteristics that tend to make a person a higher risk for suicide, and those characteristics can be identified and studied. If we were to create a "profile" of a suicidal person, it would include the following:

Age. Groups at particular risk include adolescents, college-age students, and middle-aged people of both sexes. As mentioned, the suicide rate among adolescents has tripled in the last twenty years.

Sex. Women attempt suicide three times more often than men do, but twice as many men actually succeed in committing suicide. The difference may be accounted for partly because men tend to choose more deadly methods than women do: a man is more likely to use a handgun, for example, which is quick and sure, while a woman is more likely to use sleeping pills, which is a method that allows for discovery and intervention.

Race. Blacks attempt suicide more often than members of any other race, but Caucasians are more successful at completing the suicide. Among adolescents and young adults, the rate is about even between Blacks and Caucasians; as age increases, the rate among Caucasians increases sharply. American Indians generally have the highest rate of completed suicides of any racial group in the United States, although the rate varies sharply from tribe to tribe.

Marital status. People who are married have a lower suicide rate than people who are not married (whether they have never been married, are separated, divorced, or widowed). Those who have recently lost a companion are at the highest risk for suicide. Among those who are single, the rate is highest among those who are divorced or separated and lowest among those who are widowed.

Health. Those who are ill are at a higher risk — especially if they suffer from an illness that is painful, limiting, disabling, or chronic. Those who suffer from imagined illnesses are also at risk. Any illness or surgery that changes self-image (such as a mastectomy or hysterectomy) also increases the risk for suicide.

Stress. A person who is under a significant amount of stress is at a high risk of suicide, especially if the stress stems from medical illness or the loss of a loved one. In determining what kind of stress might make a person more prone to suicide, it is important to determine the person's needs and values and his reaction to the stress. A person who is strong and independent, for example, would probably be less prone to suicide following the death of a spouse than would a person who is passive, weak, and dependent. A person who places great value on physical appearance would be more at risk for suicide following a physically disfiguring illness or accident than would a person who places greater value on intellect or personality.

Depression. The highest incidence of suicide occurs among those who are depressed — so much so, in fact, that depression is considered to be a major cause of suicide. Interestingly, suicide does not correspond with severity of depression, because suicide takes more energy than a severely depressed person can summon. As mentioned, the highest rates of suicide generally occur in the initial "recovery" phases from severe depression. Depression is especially indicative when it occurs in conjunction with insomnia, memory loss, restlessness, agitation, and feelings of helplessness or hopelessness.

Approximately 70 percent of those who attempt suicide have been diagnosed as being depressed — but you should remember that many depressed people never attempt or commit suicide, and that not all people who do commit suicide are depressed.

Recent loss. The recent loss of something important to the person places the person at higher risk for suicide. For men, the most significant loss is a loss in professional status (which includes the occurrence of retirement). For women, the most significant loss is the end of a relationship. The loss may be real or imagined. It can include such things as the loss of a loved one, the termination of a friendship, the loss of vitality or health, the loss of social status, or the loss of security.

A teenager might commit suicide after the loss of friends and social status that occurs when his family moves from one city to another; the loss of a girlfriend or boyfriend; the loss of athletic prowess; or the loss of status, such as no longer being first chair in the symphony orchestra or no longer being a member of the top-ranked debate team.

Use of drugs and/or alcohol. There are several reasons why a person who uses drugs and/or alcohol is at highest risk. First, use of drugs and alcohol indicates low impulse control in general and indicates a low tolerance for frustration and stress. Second, a person who is intoxicated or under the influence of drugs has significantly lowered control — he may act "on impulse" in a suicidal move. Third, the alcohol and drugs themselves provide the means by which to end life.

Isolation. Those who are socially isolated run a much higher risk than those who have well-structured support networks. The recent loss of a companion makes those who are isolated at an even greater risk.

Isolation plays a major factor in many adolescent suicides, when a teenager feels isolated from his peer group, his family, or others who are important in his life.

Previous suicide attempts. As discussed, those who have attempted suicide are likely to try it again; they are at a higher risk. Also at risk are those whose family members have attempted or successfully completed suicide — especially if the family member is of the same gender.

Lack of social/religious activity. People who do not enjoy any kind of activity in social or religious organizations are at a higher risk, mostly because such inactivity increases their isolation and loneliness. The specific religious group does not seem to be as important in determining risk as the level of the individual's participation in the religion.

Profession. Members of some professions are at a markedly higher risk for suicide than members of other professions. Those at higher risk include medical doctors, dentists, lawyers, and members of the helping professions (including nurses, firefighters, policemen, paramedics, and emergency medical technicians, in addition to psychologists, therapists, and psychiatrists).

Sexual preference. Homosexuals are at a higher risk for suicide than are heterosexuals.

Ability to communicate. Traditionally, those at a high risk for suicide are those who are not able to communicate their thoughts and feelings with others. People who are conditioned and able to share their joys, frustrations, sorrows, ecstasies, and concerns are less likely to commit suicide than those who are afraid to become "vulnerable" through communication.

For suicides in general — that is, among all ages — the high-risk profile would be a person who has made a previous suicide attempt; has made a direct or indirect threat of suicide; is chronically ill or isolated; is in a position of bereavement; is suffering financial stress, such as unemployment or bankruptcy; is having domestic problems, such as impending divorce or separation; is severely depressed or psychotic; has a family history of suicide; and uses alcohol, barbiturates, or hallucinogenic drugs.

Profile of the High-Risk Adolescent

Experts now believe that certain factors in our society — the lack of strong family ties, the increase in the number of broken homes, the pressures of adolescence, the increased use of alcohol and drugs, and the strong influence of movies and television — have increased the number of adolescents who are susceptible to suicide. An inability to talk about problems, the breakup of a romantic relationship, the feelings of deep depression, or the despair that comes along with missing an important opportunity can drive an adolescent to suicide over what seems like a minor problem to an adult (such as losing the championship football game). Adolescents who have existing suicidal impulses can be easily pushed over the brink, for example, by seeing a suicide on the movie screen or by hearing that someone else in town committed suicide, says Westchester Mental Health Commissioner Eugene Aronowitz, who is studying the cluster phenomenon.

City University of New York psychologists Carl F. Wells and Irving R. Stuart have identified some of the specific behaviors and factors that increase risk or indicate suicide proneness among adolescents:

Precipitating circumstances. The most common precipitating circumstance in adolescent suicide is a disciplinary crisis: often the teenager is simply anticipating discipline that will occur as a result of antisocial behavior or truancy. Thirteen-year-old Arthur, who was raised in a strict home governed by religious values, had been threatened by his parents if he ever experimented with drugs. One balmy afternoon, Arthur and three of his friends were caught by a teacher as they smoked a marijuana cigarette in the bathroom at school. The four were marched to the principal's office; after a stern lecture, the principal informed the four that he was going to call their parents and report the incident. Terrified about what might await him at home, Arthur drank a bottle of cleaning solution that he found in one of the custodial closets and curled up in the darkness to die.

Other common precipitating circumstances include a fight with peers of the same sex, a dispute with a close friend of the opposite sex, or a fight with a parent.

Age. Among adolescents, the highest risk occurs in those fifteen to twenty-four years of age. Studies show that while suicide can and does occur in children as young as three years of age, it is fairly rare among those under the age of twelve.

Sex. In the United States, twice as many teenage boys commit suicide as do teenage girls. Girls attempt suicide more often and tend to choose less letal means when they do commit suicide, which may partly account for the difference.

Intelligence. Adolescents who commit suicide tend to be extremely intelligent — even gifted — young people. High achievers with drive and a high spirit of competition tend to commit suicide more often than children who are less competitive. While adolescents who commit suicide tend to

---

"More than 90 percent of adolescents who attempt suicide think their families don't understand them. Most feel unappreciated and unloved. Their fear of failure and rejection is so great that they choose to face death rather than continue facing life."

—Brent Q. Hafen, Ph.D. and Brenda Peterson, M.S., The Crisis Intervention Handbook

have a high degree of intelligence, they also tend to have learning disorders, such as difficulties with reading.

Physical development. Just as adolescents who tend to commit suicide are precocious intellectually, they also tend to be advanced physically. In one study of adolescents who had committed suicide, one-third of the teenagers were over the seventy-fifth percentile for their height. Some researchers have suggested that the physical and hormonal changes associated with puberty may partly explain the tendency for those going through those changes to be suicidal; others dismiss the theory.

Personality/behavioral traits. Certain personality and behavioral traits seem to be more common among teenagers who commit suicide. Many felt that they were not liked by others or that others were unduly critical of them; some were described by friends and teachers as having a "chip on the shoulder." About the same percentage are described as quiet, uncommunicative, or difficult to get through to. An inability to express feelings and to ask for help seems to be a common personality trait among suicidal adolescents.

Another common personality trait is perfectionism: a teenager is methodical, driven by extremely high standards, critical of himself, and terrified of making a mistake or "not measuring up."

Craig's father had graduated from Harvard, and it had been his lifelong dream to have his son follow in his footsteps. Craig wanted nothing more than to please his father and to be accepted into Harvard's highly competitive business school, so

---

"Parents need suicide information that emphasizes the importance of the early years in a child's development, and the many subtle ways children can be made to feel unloved and unwanted."

—*Francine Klagsbrun, author of* Too Young To Die

he started in the seventh grade to work toward his goal. He kept detailed homework charts, scheduled his leisure time strictly, and spent Saturday afternoons at the library instead of sliding on the grass at the neighborhood park. As he progressed through junior high and high school, Craig exercised incredible discipline and concentration on aiming for Harvard's business school. Whenever his concerned mother suggested that he take an afternoon off to ride his bike with a few friends, he firmly refused.

At registration for his junior year, he chose all advanced-placement classes, some of which were traditionally reserved for students who were seniors. Despite Craig's discipline and obvious above-average intelligence, he had overloaded himself. He struggled into the wee hours of the morning to complete his class assignments, and he collapsed into weary sleep on the weekends.

By the time his class was scheduled to take the battery of national tests that most colleges use for entrance criteria, Craig was exhausted, depressed, and anxious. Questions in the test booklets didn't make sense; the columns of marks on the answer sheet seemed to blur together. Craig's head throbbed. He could sense that he had miserably failed the tests, and he was furious at himself for not measuring up to his own high standards. Without even waiting for the red and blue envelope

---

—*"Family stability is conducive to personal stability. A child should be taught very early to seek comfort, advice, and solace within his family. If he has no family, he should have a surrogate father or mother or friends to confide in. A child should be encouraged to express his fears, to verbalize his anger and frustration. When the child verbalizes his feelings, and sorts them, then he can understand himself and he can understand others."*

—*Aida McKellar, M.D., Assistant Professor of Psychiatry, Baylor College of Medicine*

that held the test scores to arrive in the mail, Craig steered his speeding car over a steep cliff in the nearby mountains, plummeting several hundred feet to his fiery death.

Almost opposite of teenagers like Craig are another high-risk group: those who are erratic in self-discipline, volatile and easily angered, and impulsive. These teenagers typically lack self-control, and some suicidal teenagers tend to have an antisocial problem, such as truancy, stealing, running away, or frequent fighting.

Dr. Larry Gernsbacher identified a number of personality and character traits that seem to be more commonly associated with teenagers who commit suicide. Many teenagers who commit or attempt suicide, says Dr. Gernsbacher, are proud, narcissistic, compulsive, arrogant, egocentric, perfectionistic, and irrational. He even goes so far as to say that "all" of the characteristics are present "in the personality of every suicide, regardless of how well disguised."

In addition, says Dr. Gernsbacher, teenagers who commit suicide have become alienated, usually as a result of the personality traits described above. While a teenager may try a number of things to resolve that alienation, most attempts backfire — and suicide remains the only viable option.

The personality of a teenage suicide victim may have derailed him and resulted in extreme frustration, says Dr. Gernsbacher. For example, a teenager who seeks mastery, power, and control may end up with rigidity, hostility, and arrogance. A teenager who tries to comply with others and who seeks love and altruistic goodness may end up instead feeling deprived,

---

"Children of divorce suffer, sometimes terribly. Children also suffer, sometimes even more terribly, in homes which remain intact. If the intact homes are really only superficially intact, in the long run those children may suffer as much as or more than the children of divorce."

—*Melvin G. Goldzband, M.D., Clinical Professor of Psychiatry, University of California School of Medicine, San Diego*

inadequate, and abused. A teenager who wants to gain freedom, self-sufficiency, and independence can end up feeling detached and ambivalent.

Teenagers who commit suicide tend to be depressed frequently, exhibit a sad countenance, or are often tearful. Some have excessive fears, refuse to attend school, or seem to be bored with life in general. Many suicidal teenagers are hypochondriacal — they imagine themselves to be ill, deformed, or malfunctioning.

Family background. As will be discussed later, many experts feel that an adolescent's environment is the most significant factor in the proneness to commit suicide. Helplessness and vulnerability always make a teenager more prone to suicide — and factors such as family violence, intense marital discord, or loss of a parent through death, divorce, or separation can significantly increase a child's sense of helplessness and vulnerability. In some families, a child is made to feel "bad"; as a result, he feels rejected, and he wants to die.

Teenagers who are more prone to suicide tend to have had difficulties relating to one or both of their parents. At highest risk are children who feel ambivalent toward a parent — they love the parent, but at the same time hate the parent because of exaggerated differences in personality. The ensuing guilt may cause a child to be overwhelmed by guilt for not having feelings of "unconditional love" for the parent in question.

Twelve-year-old Katy was an exuberant, energetic child who made friends easily and loved to be involved in everything that was going on around her. She was one of the first girls in town to sign up for Little League baseball, and she was the team "firecracker." She and a friend took first place in the grade school science fair, and she persuaded her father to let her take ballet lessons.

At the other end of the spectrum was Katy's mother, Martha. In the fourteen years of her marriage, Martha had suffered bouts of extreme depression; for most of Katy's life, Martha had been sullen, withdrawn, and morose. When Katy dashed into the house after school, brimming with tales of the experiment in science class or the movie that had been beamed on the wall during afternoon assembly, Martha met her with a glazed, dark expression. She rarely showed interest in Katy or her activities and actually grew to resent her for being so happy.

In the meantime, Katy's own feelings were brewing beneath the surface. Why couldn't her mother ever be happy? Why did she always cast such a sullen gloom over everything and everybody in the house? Why did she always have to ruin it? A casual observer might have expected Martha — the depressed, withdrawn one — to be the suicidal individual in the home. Instead, it was Katy who slashed her wrists one autumn morning in the solitude of the basement bathroom. Joyful, exuberant Katy could no longer live with the guilt of hating her mother.

What about the parents of suicidal children? Researchers have isolated some characteristics of parents that lead to a high risk of suicidal behavior in their children. Parents with the following characteristics significantly increase the risk of suicide in their children:

"Money and privilege buy lots of things. They buy cars. They buy instant gratification. They buy all kinds of seeming opportunities to make oneself feel fulfilled. But what is missing is that families have lost the ability to teach coping skills, to teach calmness, to teach perserverance. Everybody on this earth is going to get depressed from time to time. Everybody's going to experience grave disappointments throughout life about how they see themselves and what goals they're not going to meet. And the busier, the more intense our society is, the more people are going to be prone to grab what seem to be quick cures — drink, drugs, violence — as opposed to perservering through difficult times and doing the hard work one needs to do to sustain rich goals and relationships."

—Dr. Kim Smith, Co-Director, The Menninger Suicide Research Project

—The parents themselves have thought about suicide, threatened to commit suicide, attempted suicide, or successfully committed suicide.

—The parents are troubled by deep, clinical depression.

—There is a role reversal between parent and child because of the parent's inability to cope with the demands of parenting. The parent is overwhelmed by the duties inherent with parenthood and seems incapable of responding appropriately to the child's developmental needs. In the role reversal that results, the child is forced into a role of nurturing the parent instead of receiving nurturance from the parent.

—There is extreme disorganization in the family unit, and the parent is not able to control or handle it. In many cases, the teenager's suicide was not the only problem in the family — it was merely one of many symptoms or problems suffered by some or all of the family members.

—The parent projects himself or herself onto the child. In extreme cases, the parent is emotionally unable to distinguish himself from the child; the child is imbued with the parent's strengths, weaknesses, faults, and problems. As a result, the parent may project his feelings of rage or helplessness onto the child, who is then regarded as "bad" or "to blame."

—Parents who place their children at high risk tend to be manipulators: they threaten that they will "leave" or "commit suicide" if the child does not do as the parent wishes. Children in this kind of a situation become terrified and tend to begin responding by becoming manipulators themselves.

St. Francis Xavier University Professor Angela Gillis identifies seven family factors that place an adolescent at higher risk for suicide:

—The family is understandingly different from other families in the community. The family may have vastly different social practices, or may be active in a religious faith that others in the community do not practice. This risk becomes even greater if the parents are not able or willing to defend or explain these differences to a teenager who is struggling in an attempt to establish a values system.

—The family emphasizes material possessions or social status more than the personal growth of family members. Every child — in fact, every person — has an overwhelming need to gain approval from the significant people in his or her life. When he can't gain that approval through appropriate measures, he will use inappropriate methods. A parent who is wrapped up earning money or achieving social status may not have the time or energy to pay attention to a child — who will then interpret the lack of attention as rejection.

—The child was unwanted. The risk is highest among oldest children whose mothers were pregnant with them at the time of marriage. Why? Such a child may go through life feeling "repressed ambivalence" of his mother, according to Ms. Gillis.

—Both parents in the family work, without giving the children enough love and attention. Such parents may also delegate adult responsibility to children who are not ready to asssume it — and may even force the children into a role of "parent," not only for other children in the family, but for themselves as well.

—Parents in the family use rejection or threat as a way of getting the children to cooperate. The result? The adolescent grows up with the deep-seated fear that he never really measured up to his parents' expectations of him.

—Parents neglect or abuse their children because of inadequate parenting skills; the neglect and abuse may be either physical or emotional in nature. In addition to lacking technical parenting skills, such as how to feed or care for a baby, some parents also lack emotional skills because they were never cared for or loved themselves. It is difficult to express those emotions for a child when the emotions are foreign!

—"Only" children are at risk because many only children do not develop an adequate sense of self-worth. If the child's parents were older when she was born, she may also feel an overwhelming burden for setting the emotional tone in the family.

—Depression. Until recently, depression was thought to be an adult problem; most researchers refused to believe that children as young as two or three could be overcome by feelings of severe depression. Clinical research involving children has now proven that children do indeed suffer; common symptoms include poor appetite, weight loss, sleep difficulty, sadness, excessive guilt, poor concentration, loss of interest, and thoughts of death or suicide.

A child who feels depressed is at a significantly higher risk of suicide than a child who does not feel depressed. Emotions that particularly characterize suicidal children include feelings of hopelessness, feelings of worthlessness, overwhelming sadness, withdrawal, and wishes to die.

Factors at birth. Startling new research indicates that some adolescents may be more vulnerable to suicide during their teenage years because of certain factors present at birth. Dr. Lee Salk, professor of psychology and psychiatry and professor of pediatrics at The New York Hospital - Cornell Medical Center in New York City, conducted the studies — and he says that while the birth factors do not necessarily *lead to* teenage suicide, they can put a teenager at much higher risk.

"Lifestyle means changing social and economic factors. Lifestyle means more mothers having to work today. It means more children at home alone because of inadequate day-care. It means placing youngsters in the custody of others. It means changes in the family, less extended family support, changes in diet, greater stress, and more susceptibility to forces like advertising, television, alcohol, and drugs."

—Dr. J. Larry Brown, Executive Director, Harvard School of Public Health

---

He pinpointed three birth factors that seem to increase suicide risk: (1) being born to a mother who had no prenatal care for the first twenty weeks (five months) of the pregnancy; (2) being born to a mother who had chronic disease during pregnancy; and (3) suffering respiratory distress for more than one hour at birth. According to Dr. Salk, only 11.5 to 19.3 percent of the general population have one or more of these

"I see nothing but conflicts
No meaning to life.
Yet no meaning to death.

Time passes by
Minute by minute, hour by hour
As I see myself die.
No one around to relieve my loneliness
No one around me who cares.
Each day that passes
I see nothing but conflicts.
No meaning to life,
Yet no meaning to death.
I'm like a rope in tug-of-war
Always being pulled upon.
Constant anger
But all inside,
As I see myself die.
Never any happiness
Only hopelessness and helplessness.
Shall the day arrive soon
Or shall I survive.
How can I live with a constant lie,
For . . ., she must die."

—*Written by a seventeen-year-old high school student currently undergoing psychotherapy for depression.*

three factors; approximately 60 percent of the teenagers who commit suicide have one or more.

There is some explanation for the increase in vulnerability due to these factors, says Dr. Salk. A baby who suffers respiratory distress for more than an hour at birth may have sustained some neurologic damage that can impair his ability to deal with the stresses of life. Such a baby may also have actually suffered clinical death before being resuscitated — and, like adults who have experienced a near-death incident, may have a diminished fear of death.

The other factors — lack of prenatal care or chronic disease during pregnancy — can also affect the child. A mother who does not seek prenatal care may very probably be suffering from an unwanted pregnancy — a message she may later convey (consciously or subconsciously) to the child. A mother who suffers from a chronic disease during pregnancy may very realistically have a difficult time relating to that child throughout the rest of its life.

The "birth factor" ideas are just that — a new theory that has not been adequately verified.

Distorted concept of death. At a high risk for suicide is the child or teenager who does not have a clear understanding of death: the child does not believe that death is permanent but instead sees it as a reversible and temporary state of pleasantness in which to escape problems. The child may see death almost as a gentle, nurturing experience or a way in which to have wishes granted, not as a permanent, final condition from which one never returns.

Break with reality. Children who do not have a firm grasp on reality are at a significantly higher risk for suicide than children who do. A teenager may perceive that he is failing at school when, in fact, he is doing well. Another teenager may be terrified by her imagined rejection by friends when, in fact, the friends accept her openly and easily. Those who suffer a major break with reality tend to be overcome by disappointment and frustration and lose the ability to adapt and cope with everyday problems.

Desire to manipulate. At extremely high risk is the child who, caught in an abusive or extraordinarily unpleasant situation, feels an overwhelming desire to take control of the situation in which he feels helpless, vulnerable, and enraged. In such a situation, the teenager may begin to fantasize: he may think about what his suicide would do to those who are oppressing him, or he may think about the pleasantness of joining loved ones who are dead.

Jerry was a twelve-year-old who was caught in such a situation: his father was an abusive alcoholic, and his mother took out her own feelings of helplessness and victimization on Jerry. At its best, the atmosphere in the home was tense; at its worst, it exploded with violence. Jerry would often cower beneath the layers of quilting that separated him from the frosty winter air in his attic bedroom, dreaming of what it would be like if his parents found him dead. He would create elaborate scenes in his mind in which his father, reeling with inebriation, would be suddenly sobered by the bloodied corpse and in which his mother would torment herself with guilt over all the hateful things she had done. One April morning, after carefully rehearsing the scene in his mind for months, Jerry calmly walked to a fourth-floor window in his English class at the junior high school, slid his legs over the smooth sill, and jumped to his death on the smooth concrete below.

"There are many types of youth who may be a ~isk for suicide. Some may be angry, impulsive and in trouble. Others may be perfectionistic and compulsive, leading to disappointment that impairs their ability to cope. Yet, the most common factor is serious depression, which increasingly is present at younger ages. It is important to know what behaviors may suggest that someone is at risk.

—Youth Suicide National Center

Adolescent Development

Critical to an understanding of adolescent suicide is an understanding of the emotional demands associated with adolescent development. Researcher Barbara Varenhorst, director of the Palo Alto Peer Counseling Program in conjunction with the National Institute on Drug Abuse, part of the U.S. Department of Health and Human Services' Alcohol, Drug Abuse, and Mental Health Administration, has isolated some of the factors regarding adolescents and the society in which they live that help provide an understanding of the many pressures encountered during the teenage years. This chapter is an overview of that work.

What *is* it like to be an adolescent in the United States today? Is today's teenager different from the one who grew up two or three generations ago? Most important, is adolescence really a distinct period of development, or is it primarily a stage of life that we have "created?"

The answers are difficult to find. Research is conflicting and incomplete, and interpretations of the data differ, according to who is making the interpretations. Unfortunately, much of the research has been done on teenagers representing only the lowest or highest socioeconomic classes in our society, on deviant or troubled youth, basically with older teenagers, and primarily with boys. But even with these handicaps in research, some very valuable and useful information has been sifted out about what it is like to be an adolescent.

One thing we *do* know, but frequently forget, is that adolescents are people — not categories. They are young people who are anticipating their futures, experiencing problems with relationships, and wanting and needing recognition, respect, and guidance from parents, peers, and society. They are human beings, not stereotypes or faceless groups to be classified by researchers. Therefore, it is important to differentiate between the adolescent *person* and a period of life called *adolescence*.

If you were asked to describe adolescents, what would you say? What images immediately come to mind? What feelings surface when you think about adolescents? Do you smile — or shudder? Is the image that comes to mind a "problem" — or is it the unique things about these young people, such as their music, hairstyles, clothes, and eating habits?

How you answer these questions might illustrate how well you understand adolescents and what kinds of myths you believe about them. Many of the common myths about adolescents are negative, and they prejudice our thinking; more serious, those myths influence the way in which we treat teenagers. Some of the myths create a deep distrust and even dislike for young people during some of the most critical years of their lives; as a result, we too often treat them with either benign neglect or approach them as though we always expect a crisis. On the one hand, we tend to look at them as "silly" children; on the other hand, we see them as dangerous monsters. Strangled by these myths, we tend to jump to the conclusion that teenagers are always planning something bad or are always involved in negative activities.

Common Myths About Adolescents

Adolescents are not quite "normal." Too many believe that adolescents are merely going through a stress and storm period in life, which tends to be pathological, but that they usually grow out of it. Because of this myth, we automatically expect problems from teenagers. One researcher says that this myth fosters an attitude that essentially says, "Be good, have fun, stay out of trouble, prepare for life, and we'll get back to you later when you are normal, we like you better, and we understand you more." Yet because teenagers are so self-critical already, any adult suggestion of "abnormality" only intensifies their fears. They don't need further criticism or worry; they need adults who will calm them down and explain the normality of what is happening to them.

Adolescence is a transitional period of life, and, therefore, it is a temporary and less significant or "real" stage of living. The label "transitional" is a type of put-down. Young people don't feel that they are transitional or temporary. What they are doing and going through is of intense importance to them. The here-and-now is what determines their needs, their growth, and their self-concepts.

Adolescents are basically all alike. You can't find a more widely variable group in our society than adolescents! Parents who have had more than one child know this, and so do teachers who work with teenagers. Yet most people react as though all adolescents are the same. It is damaging and misleading to generalize to all youth the behaviors, problems, and characteristics exhibited by just a few. It is especially damaging if the few are troubled adolescents whose problems and behaviors are vividly advertised by the media. This myth has been responsible for the belief that there is a generation gap between youth and adults. Some youth *do* have problems relating to an older person, but many do not. The specific differences among adolescents will be discussed later, and they are as real and as pronounced as the specific differences among a wide group of adults or children.

Every adolescent is growing in a uniform, continuous, scheduled pattern. This is one of the most dangerous of the myths, because it affects the expectations that adults have of adolescents. Like other myths, it is completely untrue. Just as there are differences among adolescents, so there are great variations in the types and levels of growth happening at a particular time. Unfortunately, biological, social, emotional, and intellectual growth are not synchronized. For example, a boy who is tall for his age may not be emotionally mature. An early-maturing girl may still enjoy collecting dolls, reading children's books, and even sitting on her father's knee. Physical development often triggers adults' expectations of a corresponding social and emotional maturity. These inappropriate expectations create problems that can affect young people's futures.

Adolescents are still children. If this myth were true, it would mean that adolescents are not capable of responsibility, decision-making, serious thought or conversation, or any type of independence. It is *not* true, however; adolescents are capable of all those things!

If the myths were untrue, then what are the facts?

Because of the tasks, challenges, and new experiences the adolescent encounters, adolescence is an exhilarating developmental period of tremendous significance. It can be a stressful period, both for adolescents and adults. Identifying the tasks and challenges that are natural — as opposed to those that we have artificially created — has been the work of a number of social scientists. There are a number of theories, and a variety of definitions.

If we were to consolidate the theories and the definitions, we would say that adolescence is a period spanning the time from the changes of puberty to full adult physical growth. The end of adolescence is usually marked by such events as getting a full-time job, establishing autonomy in relationship to parents, and entering stable, mature relationships that often involve marriage and child-rearing. Even those criteria for "passage" into adult life do not always hold true: today's young people are going to school longer, delaying or avoiding marriage, and finding it increasingly difficult to get full-time jobs even when they are ready and desire to do so. The only specific and unchanging rites of passage into adult life that we provide at specific times are voting rights, legal ages for buying alcohol and tobacco, the right to enter into a legal contract, and so on.

Theories of Adolescence

Over the years, some significant theories of adolescence have emerged that are helpful in understanding what teenagers must do to become competent, independent adults. One of the best-known theorists, Erik Erikson, believes that adolescence is a time of both an identity crisis and a psychosocial moratorium. Adolescence is the first time that most of us realize we have a unique past and future; it's a time for "re-grouping" — or, as many teenagers say — "getting your act together." Such re-grouping involves thinking about the future, beginning to solidify who one is, and establishing a more stable values system.

Supposedly, this "moratorium" is a period of time delay granted by society to people at the end of childhood before they have to make adult commitments. Erikson believes that it is a necessary and important time of socially approved exploration and experimentation; if blocked, he says, it can lead to a premature foreclosure of identity development.

Other researchers don't agree: they argue that adolescents are *not* given the right to explore and experiment. They do agree that adolescents in America have difficulty finding a prescribed niche for themselves in the adult world.

The Tasks Facing An Adolescent

Regardless of which theory you believe, one thing stands true: the adolescent must work through a number of "tasks," must accomplish a number of transitions, before he enters into adulthood.

Becoming physically sexually mature. This is a major, basic task, and it is a universal one — in other words, every adolescent on the face of the earth has to mature sexually before he becomes an adult. For most young people, the years from twelve to sixteen are the most eventful years of their lives as far as growth and development are concerned. Early adolescence is second only to infancy in terms of growth.

The development of sexual maturity is a phenomenon that belongs only to adolescence. Biologically, it is a totally new experience for the adolescent. Its significance is due partly to the fact that it happens to everyone and partly because it carries with it changing expectations from others and from oneself.

While it is happening, the young person is a fascinated spectator of the developments or lack of developments that are taking place, which either charm or horrify the adolescent. At this time, feelings emerge of realizing that one has something in common with all human beings, causing a new assessment of the world around oneself. This awakening affects relationships with peers and with adults.

Developing individuality. The adolescent has plenty to explore: "Who am I?" "What do my relationships mean to me?" As young people find answers to their questions, their preferences, interests, and personalities begin to blossom. It is a time when the teenager's self-concept is solidified and tested. This involves becoming aware of the continuity of oneself from

---

"The path to adulthood is a rocky one to climb unaided. It can be frustrating, disappointing — and depressing. Indeed, for adolescents, depression seems to go with the territory. In a study of 5,600 high school youngsters, depression was shown to be second only to colds, sore throats, and coughs in frequency."

—*Charlotte P. Ross, President/Executive Director, Youth Suicide National Center*

one moment to the next, of sorting out past experiences and integrating them into an awareness of the future. It is a sensitive and fragile task, but while going through it, one is preparing for another task — making a commitment to the future.

Forming commitments. As children move toward adulthood, they need to learn how to get along with others and how to contribute to the world around them. To do this, they need to explore a purpose in life, a reason for living, and a vocational choice. Young people accomplish this by experimenting with wider circles of life, meeting various kinds of people, seeing other cultures, and participating in some aspects of the adult work world. They also need chances to experiment with their own strengths and values, and they need opportunities to participate as citizens, as members of households, and as workers and responsible people in society. We don't provide many chances for them to do this — at least we don't offer them consistently. Why? Too often we still see adolescents as children, and, therefore, as either irresponsible or dangerous. We need to allow youth to experiment without suffering disastrous consequences when they fail or make mistakes. We need to let them try out some paths of life without having to make irrevocable commitments.

If experimentation is to be healthy, however, youth also need to be held responsible for their actions and accountable for the impact that they have on other human beings. Providing for this dual kind of experimentation requires a fine line of

"Our daughters are being asked to find out who they are in a culture that is in itself having a severe identity crisis. Caught between the traditional world of mother and the new frontier of freedom, they're propelled toward fulfilling all possibilities the changing world offers. It's an impossible goal that is taking its toll."

—*Janet Chase*, Daughters of Change: Growing Up in America

judgment and guidance from adults, which is often difficult to provide.

Gaining separation and forming autonomy. This is one of the most difficult tasks for both teenagers and adults to accomplish. Withdrawing from and escaping adult protection is difficult — difficult for the teenager, and distressing for the parents. It involves the healthy and necessary move away from family and toward peers. Separation is a lifelong process, but the egg is cracked during adolescence as young people begin to move outward beyond the home and parents for their opinions, clothing styles, values, and authorities. We often misread the signals that young people give about their progressive need for detachment, however, as well as their continuing need for adults to set limits. It's important not just to read the signals accurately, but to handle one's own reaction to the process of separation. Often parents experience feelings of a reduced sense of prestige and a certain amount of loss of control — something that is tremendously unsettling to parents. Some react by thinking that everything is up for grabs; others react by clamping down with inappropriate controls. Still others immediately give up and turn over complete freedom to their children.

When a child experiences unrestricted freedom, the quality of the autonomy he has achieved is questionable. Some question whether achieving such easy freedom interferes with a

---

"A child should also be taught that he can be the cause of violence in others — that certain actions on his part can provoke anger in others, namely teasing, nagging, or disrespect of others. He should be taught courtesy and consideration toward his fellow men. A child raised in love, self-respect, warmth, and security will develop strength to face violence."

—*Aida McKellar, M.D., Assistant Professor of Psychiatry, Baylor College of Medicine*

---

teenager's ability to achieve emotional and value separation from adults. That kind of "cheap" autonomy might actually interfere with a teenager's ability to eventually become a truly independent adult. Nature provides a perfect example: a moth must go through the struggle of breaking out of the restrictions of the cocoon in order to develop the strength to fly and survive. If the struggle is necessary for the moth, it might also be necessary for us.

The peer group, so important to adolescents, is often seen as the embodiment of evil. A major factor in today's family problems is parental distrust of their children's friends and suspicion about what is happening when they are together. The peer group is essential — a reliable prediction of future delinquent behavior is a young person's inability to function in a peer group. The peer group is the lifeline for an adolescent — but adults in his life are also an important lifeline. Because of that, it is essential that adults not set themselves up in competition with the peer group or in opposition to it but in support and tandem instead. Serious consequences result when either the parents (adults) or the peer group is cut off.

Outgrowing types of egocentrism. Two main kinds of "egocentrism" are typical of adolescence. One is the feeling that you are always on stage, that everyone is always looking at you, listening to you, and judging you. While it is often painful, it is a kind of self-importance that must be worked through. The self-involvement that accompanies it is most obvious in the adolescent's preoccupation with his own body and its physical changes.

The second kind of egocentrism is a kind of psychological loneliness in which the adolescent pines, "I am alone; no one understands me; I am unique; what happens to me doesn't happen to anyone else." Part of it often includes a kind of immortality in which the teenager believes he will never die, he will never fail, she will not become pregnant, or he will never become addicted to drugs.

Self-analysis is necessary and helpful in discovering who you are, but it can become destructive if there is too much occupation with self. The general attitude among all ages of "finding oneself" makes it even more difficult for adolescents to work successfully through the period of egocentrism and to learn to reflect on themselves in relation to others.

Reevaluating values. All of life involves the process of learning and formulating values. But the major work on values formation is done during adolescence. Why? An adolescent is beginning to develop the capacity to think beyond the concrete to abstractions of life, and is experiencing a wider exposure to people and to the things life has to offer. During this developmental period, children gradually begin to be able to deal with cognitive challenges that make it possible to form independent moral judgments.

The kind of questioning that adolescents go through during this period is often irritating and scary for adults, since the teenager starts questioning the values of the adults around him. But this questioning is normal and necessary for human development. Independent adults have had to go through the process of evaluating thoughts, feelings, beliefs, and ethics. For young people to do this, they need a stable set of values against which their emerging personal values can be tested. Given the inconsistency of values that we as adults display in our behavior, our institutions, and our words, youth today are finding it harder to weigh values and choose the ones that will guide them.

Society's current inconsistency about values also increases the power of peer group pressure. The peer group is a natural

---

"Adolescents need touch to facilitate communication and convey caring. When children are no longer held and comforted by their parents, they may turn to their peers instead. There is almost no data on this, but I wonder if the increase in very young teenager pregnancy comes from the need to be held. They may be using sex for a nonsexual purpose."

—*Dr. Elizabeth R. McAnarney, Director of Adolescent Medicine at the University of Rochester Medical School*

source of information about values. As a teenager chooses and deals with friends, she learns new values and is forced into assessing old ones. If the values of adults around her are vague, fluid, or contradictory, she will depend even more heavily on her equally confused, still immature peers. Perhaps some of the greatest problems that we face with youth today — such as teenage pregnancy and drug abuse, not to mention suicide — are products of this confusion. A teenager needs guidelines if he is to establish a solid base for his personal value systems.

The Adolescent Who Needs Attention

The early adolescent — the child between the ages of twelve and fifteen — is the most understudied, least understood, and most ineffectively served group in the entire population. That's a tragedy, because during early adolescence the most dramatic changes happen to the body, the sharpest shifts in social adjustment take place, and a new set of confusing expectations occur. All this creates tremendous emotional anxiety, which requires understanding and constructive help. It is critical that we realize what is "normal" about adolescents and what their needs are:

Sexual development belongs almost entirely to the early adolescent. *When* sexual maturity occurs is a factor that critically affects the development of the teenager's self-esteem, personal identity, and performance in school. It also affects the expectations of the teenager's parents and teachers. An important factor is whether the teenager is a boy or a girl: in our society, it is a distinct advantage for boys if they mature early, but a disadvantage for girls.

Why? Early-maturing boys are often given more leadership roles, are more popular, excel in athletic ability, and are seen as being more attractive by adults and peers. (This even carries over into late adolescence, where studies show that early-maturing boys are more self-confident, less dependent, and better able to assume more adult roles in interpersonal relations.) Boys who mature late, however, show more personal and social maladjustments through adolescence. Significant numbers of late-maturing boys have negative self-concepts, are more rebellious toward parents, and often feel profound rejection from their peers.

Early-maturing girls, on the other hand, develop feelings of being the "odd one out." Many of their female peers and most of their male classmates have not matured. They often develop submissive, indifferent social behavior and lack social poise. Research shows that these girls have little influence on their peer group and are seldom seen as being popular or admired, or as leaders. Late-maturing girls, however, are, on the average, more outgoing and assured during early adolescence and later become confident, poised aaoiescents who are frequently seen as leaders.

It is not just the time of maturation that creates these personality characteristics and self-images — rather, it is the reaction of peers and adults and the understanding that they have of what is happening and why. One of the prime concerns of early adolescents is, "Am I normal?" Another is, "How acceptable are these changes to others?" A simple service that adults can provide is a better understanding of the facts regarding what is going on, what is normal, and what will be happening before the process of becoming an adult is completed.

External situations and factors often make the stress of adjusting to physical maturation even more intense. One of these is the social setting of the junior high school: theoretically, the junior high school was designed to ease the transition from a self-contained classroom with one interested, involved teacher to the larger world of the high school. In fact, however, the junior high school, and to a great extent the middle school, is just a duplication of the patterns of high school. So the transition is not eased, but intensified, because it now comes earlier in a young person's life. As it works out, the entry to junior high school occurs at the same time as the significant changes of puberty in most girls. Expectations of academic performances increase sharply at this time, even though the cognitive development of junior high students is inadequate to meet this demand. While the adolescent's social world is expanding, he or she is also faced with more complicated and demanding expectations. When all of these adjustments are superimposed on one period of life — one that is still wobbly in terms of coping skills — it is a major crossroads of development. The wonder is that so many early adolescents do so well and actually survive.

Parents often complicate these adjustments because they see going into junior high school as a rite of passage. It is at this time that they begin to treat their children differently and to hold different standards for their behavior — now they are "adolescents." Unfortunately, some parents also begin to expect problems, especially with peers and peer pressure. In some ways, of course, the expectation is realistic. As younger adolescents begin the separation process, they develop feelings of ambivalence toward their parents, and this often results in rebellious behavior. As the loyalties of young teenagers shift from their parents to their peers, outbursts are frequent, arguments are intense, and differences of opinion can be extreme. Rebelliousness is primarily a trait of the early adolescent, however, not of adolescents as a whole.

Egocentrism reaches its peak during early adolescence. The more egocentric a teenager is, the less objective he can be. The junior high school student often is not yet able to generalize, to use symbols, or to process information with objectivity. Most have not yet matured enough to go beyond concrete approaches to learning. Because of this, they are often "typed" as being difficult to teach. Their lack of objectivity and their excessive involvement with themselves makes them inconsiderate of others and difficult to engage in an extensive conversation. Parents and teachers who don't take the level of maturity into consideration may hold out unrealistic expectations that the teenager is not capable of meeting. Then, when the teenager can't meet the expectations, she feels inadequate, which fuels her already-heightened sense of self-criticism.

Contrast these conditions with the circumstances of the high school-age adolescent. Older adolescents have no distinctive new adjustments or changes in status to endure. Most have completed their physical growth and development. Their interpersonal relationships are more mature and constructive, and they are more highly critical in their evaluation of their peers. They are experimenting and learning new roles, but they plan and choose more thoughtfully. Having done some exploratory learning about the opposite sex, they are able to enter into more nurturing relationships based on mutual trust and an element of tenderness. When a person reaches high school, he has usually attained full cognitive development. This makes it possible to deal with contradictory aspects of the world, to accept some of the deficiencies of parents, to make moral decisions, and to consider a tentative vocational commitment. The late adolescent is able to consider others, and wants to. Finally, there is the desire and longing to take part in decision-making, to shoulder responsibilities, and to have a say in one's own destiny.

Social and Cultural Factors Affecting Adolescents

Adolescence is also the time when young people encounter some of the barriers that adults have created to completing the process of healthy development. The teenager becomes vulnerable to some of society's external factors and events. A number of those events are shaping the lives of today's adolescents. Three major changes stand out when you consider the external factors that affect teenagers: *the changing structure of families; the weakened tie between children and their parents and the increasing importance of the peer group; and the surrender of major responsibilities to schools, social services, and agencies.* There are other factors — the increased specialization of the job skills requiring higher levels of education; technological developments that have reduced the value of teenage labor (and that have therefore reduced the chances for teenagers to learn about adult work roles); and the constant influence and presence of television, which often competes with parents as a source of values and morals. But as important as all these are, none is as critical as the changes in the family, the dominance of the peer group, and the delegation of developmental functions to agencies outside the home.

What have these changes produced? — Greater behavioral freedom for teenagers without having to be accountable; greater demands for social competence without systematic instruction; heavier peer pressure, with less self-esteem to resist it; and more pursuit of pleasure and escape through drugs and sex without the awareness of more helpful alternatives. But, perhaps most important, these changes have resulted in a profound loneliness that is different, more abnormal, and more pervasive than the kind that should be expected during adolescence.

A study of youth has revealed five distinct "cries" — loneliness, family trouble, prejudice, social protest, and joy. When the study was repeated ten years later, there was significant change in only two of the cries: the cry of social protest was weaker, and the cry of loneliness has become much more intense. Other researchers support those findings. Paul Zimbardo calls our time "the age of indifference. The Devil's strategy for our times is to trivialize human existence and to isolate us from one another while creating the delusion that the

---

"The rise in the suicide rate, unwanted pregnancies, and homicide in the young parallels the divorce rate, the unemployment rate, and the fragmentation of the family."

—Dr. Derek Miller, *Chief of the Adolescent Program, Northwestern Memorial Hospital's Institute of Psychiatry*

reasons are time pressures, work demands, or economic anxieties." As a result, he says, American teenagers are passively accepting a way of life that they view as empty and meaningless. This syndrome includes a constricted expression of emotions, a low threshhold of boredom, and an apparent absence of joy in anything that is not immediately consumable — which explains the importance to teenagers of music, drugs, alcohol, sex, and status-symbol possessions. This syndrome also explains why cult leaders have been so successful in wooing teenagers: they offer simple solutions to complex problems by love-bombing affection-starved teenagers. They work not on political or religious or economic ideology, but by offering the illusion of friendship and noncontingent love — "You exist, you are one of us, you get your fair share of our love and respect." That's the kind of message we used to expect to come from parents.

The resulting loneliness can drive a young person into delinquency, drug use, and self-destruction: loneliness is the most common denominator in teenage suicides.

The resulting loneliness — and its accompanying deep yearning for love and relationships — may also increase teenage sexual activity and pregnancies. According to *Newsweek*, nearly half of the nation's fifteen- to nineteen-year-old girls have had premarital sex. More than one million teenagers become pregnant each year in the United States, and almost 30,000 of them involve girls under the age of fifteen. Paula Duke, a professor in adolescent medicine at Stanford University, found some startling information about teenage sexual activity. In talking with girls who are sexually active, she found that most

---

"Parents sometimes are so busy working hard to provide the material things that they've neglected what the child really needs and wants — time, attention, love, and affection. The child acts out with suicide attempts to get attention."

—Willie Hamlin, Washington, D.C., Psychiatrist

do not seem to enjoy it — the girls express the desire for the closeness of being held, of having someone who cares about them and someone to care about, but the sexual act itself is not enjoyable. It would appear, then, that if a girl feels alone in a noncaring, friendless world, sex education is not going to turn the tide on sexual activity.

Family Changes and Parenting

Of all the changes that have occurred in family life over the past fifty years, one thing seems most critical: families are on their own, having surrendered most of their socialistic influence to various other social institutions and social groups. The American family has essentially shed in-laws, grandparents, cousins, aunts, and boarders. It has handed production over to offices and factories; religion to the churches; the administration of justice to the courts; formal education to the schools; and medical attention to the hospitals. It has in the process been stripped down to the bare frame of being marriage-centered and child-fulfilled. This parceling out of responsibilities has caused some things to be done poorly, and some things not to be done at all. The implications of this phenomenon are serious, especially when we know that services for youth are more successful when parents are intimately involved in the programs or services.

Although those changes are serious, another change is even more important: the change in parenting and child-rearing styles. Research has shown that among all the factors affecting the adolescent in the context of the family (such as the loss of an extended family, the reduction of economic cooperation, the cycle of divorce and remarriage, the changes in women's roles, and the more equal relationship between husband and wife), the most important factor in a child's psychological development is the parenting style of the available parent.

A number of teenagers cry out about family trouble — and those who feel that they have family trouble are distressed over the lack of communication with parents and the lack of understanding between themselves and their parents. They are often chagrined about being treated "like children" and are disappointed by their parents' distrust or rejection of them and their friends. Usually, these teenagers say that their parents communicate by nagging, criticizing their friends, expressing suspicion, and giving orders. Instead of treating them as someone they respect, their parents invade their privacy and overcontrol their actions. All of it combines to destroy relationships.

There are other common factors that seem to bother teenagers. Their parents are overly strict — and, instead of discussing problems, the parents communicate only by "yelling." The result? The teenager loses personal self-regard and suffers an increase in a sense of guilt. The teenager also yearns for personal freedom and independence.

One study pointed out a startling fact: parents who distrust their child bring on nineteen times a greater chance of family disunity than if there was a divorce. *Teenagers who don't have the trust of their parents are more susceptible to group pressures and are more likely to feel the loneliness that leads to suicide.*

Peer Group Factors

Adults often distrust the adolescent's peer group, bemoan peer pressures, and criticize the friends that a teenager chooses — yet some researchers contend that negligent or extreme parenting styles are what force adolescents into precocious or extreme loyalty and identification with a peer group. The family, in other words, pushes the adolescent out — the pull of the peer group alone is not enough.

One of the most disturbing trends over the past three decades is the decline in the amount of time parents and children spend together. In the absence of substantial adult participation in child rearing and direction of peer relations, peer groups may actually handicap a teenager's moral growth and development.

The tragedy of all this is that adolescents often acknowledge their lack of competence in dealing with peer groups. Among the most intense needs of teenagers is the need to learn how to make friends and be a friend. Adolescents want opportunities that allow them to take leave of their public postures, to remove their masks, to trust, to love, and to care about themselves and others. As one researcher says, friends are to young people what bread is to the hungry and clothes are to the naked.

Educational Conditions

Except for the family, the school has the greatest influence on youth. The school is where young people have opportunities for social contact with peers and adults, in addition to other kinds of learning. Yet for many adolescents, schools are not pleasant or supportive places to be. Young people in schools often experience racism and other forms of domination, severe and sometimes cruel competition and lack of understanding, and disinterested teachers and counselors. Too often schools fail to

"Although not all of the causes of our youngsters' suicidal feelings and actions are understood, we do know that for any individual despairing child, they may include feelings of loss, of failure, of hopelessness, of unimportance in the family and community, of separateness and lack of confidence in the future. We suspect that social changes may have deprived youngsters of the traditional support systems associated with home, family and community. Other factors such as expectations of parents, of teachers or of the child himself, may also play a part."

—*Youth Suicide National Center*

adjust their programs and services to the maturational or intellectual needs of their students. Chronological age is still the basic factor used to group and educate all students, and too few students are offered alternatives to this traditional model of education. Junior high schools are particularly at fault — most are totally inadequate at meeting the social and emotional needs of students, and they stress the students' subordinate status by feeding them a watered-down diet of weak-kneed "real stuff."

Too often, schools emphasize subject matter to the exclusion of the development of personal qualities — values, motives, and patterns of social response.

What Teenagers Need the Most

What, then, do adolescents need the most during this period of transition and growth?

Increased respect from adults. Young people need to be seen as significant human beings who are able and eager to participate, to contribute, and to accept responsibilities as members of society. Refusing to recognize this need is a violation of their worth, and a violation of their chances of becoming healthy adults.

More time and involvement from adults. Any adult who really cares about and is interested in young people can become a very important person to a teenager. There is no way to put a price on the help that adults provide when they voluntarily, caringly share their time with young people.

More constructive opportunities to experiment with life. We as adults must create more ways in which we can legitimately use the special talents and expertise of young people. They need not only feel that they are helping to support and conduct the business of society, but they also need better ways of being initiated into work roles. Even the opportunities for part-time work experiences for youth appear to be increasingly limited. Creative solutions to this problem must be found.

More help in developing social competence. In a more complex, sophisticated world, with fewer opportunities to learn from adult models, isolated and confined to a peer group, young people need help in learning how to cope and survive. Today it is easier for youth to learn how to work with a computer than to learn how to get along with people. Do we want to pay the price that this ultimately will demand? High on the list of competencies that youth need and want is learning how to be a caring person, how to reach out and help a friend who needs a friend.

More qualified adult youth leaders. We often assign and allow incompetent, ill-equipped adults to work with youth, giving them prime time to touch young people's lives. Again, we may be paying a high price for such neglect. Essential qualities of adults who are given the opportunity to lead and guide young people should include acceptance of youth as equals in society; knowledge and understanding of the great variety of their abilities and aspirations; the capacity to show deep respect and love for youth; and the ability to believe in youth and let them play a significant part in their programs, their decisions, and their world.

More opportunities for ethical development. It is significant that the social protest cry has become weaker during the past ten years: society's failure to involve youth in shaping the quality of life and to guide youth in reflecting on their experiences and decisions is limiting their ethical development. An ethical life may seem old-fashioned, but the future quality of American society may depend on more attention being given to the ethical development of adolescents.

Help in finding the meaning of life. Examining the meaning of life is what living is all about, and should be at the core of young people's activities and experiences. Young girls are at particular risk — young women today are growing up in a period in which many traditional roles or myths are no longer valid, and many wonder what they should believe in and reject. This search, common to so many adolescents, often expresses itself in desperate behavior, in a hopeless shrug of the shoulder, in a drowning in alcohol, or in angry outbursts. Yet the desire to participate in the world and to have a part in their own destinies remains strong.

Factors Affecting the Onset of Problem Behavior

A number of factors common to adolescent development and growth may, under certain circumstances, lead to problem behavior. The most ordinary of these factors include low self-esteem, impulsiveness, negative attitudes about school, low cognitive development, low academic aspirations, school discipline problems, delinquent or antisocial behavior, frequent use of alcohol/tobacco/drugs, poor parent/child relationships, impulsiveness, irresponsibility, and rebelliousness.

But how can we know when factors that are associated with problem behavior might actually lead to problem behavior? In a pure cause-and-effect sense, that is difficult to determine. But three variables occur consistently in relation to problem behavior:

Stress. Youth experience stress in a variety of forms: loss (of a parent or friend), rejection, abuse (sexual, emotional, or physical), and failure in varying degrees of severity and across different aspects of their experience. At-risk teenagers are highly stressed; although all youth inevitably experience some stress, those with lower levels of stress appear to be less inclined toward problem behavior.

Some of the most common stresses in children and adolescents after the age of eight were identified at the recent

National Conference on Youth Suicide. The most common stresses that lead to increased suicide risk include the birth of a sibling (more than 70 percent of suicidal children are firstborn, so they had a secondborn child with which to deal); a change in the family structure; changes in the extended family structure (such as the death of a grandparent); temporary and permanent separation, or divorce; remarriage; and changes in the home in a way that affect the kind of nurturance and care that the child is receiving. That's an important distinction: a child may not be at a higher suicidal risk because of a changed home situation if the level of nurturance and caring is kept the same or enhanced.

Skill deficiencies. Young people vary according to the kinds of skills they have for coping successfully with stress when it occurs. Important developmental skills relate to such tasks and life events as problem-solving, communication, accurate self-assessment, and constructive processes for interpreting and understanding experiences. At-risk teenagers are often characterized by low attainment of such skills. Some youth who have adequate life-coping skills can deal effectively with high degrees of stress; others who lack such skills are more vulnerable.

Situational constraints. At the situational level, the influence of the peer group is particularly important. Many teenagers' peers or role models encourage experimentation with high-risk behaviors such as substance abuse, precocious sexual activity, and vandalism. At-risk teenagers often find themselves in situations where problem behavior is expected and supported.

No one factor by itself is either necessary or sufficient to produce problem behavior; rather, it appears that the combination of varieties and degrees of factors produces a range of problem behavior of varying severity.

Factors That Contribute To Teenage Suicide

Adolescents suffer from many of the same problems that adults do, especially in a society that has exposed adolescents to many adult pressures and stresses. Some of the most common causes revolve around family situations, environmental factors, social problems, depression, developmental factors, and other factors associated with adolescence.

Family Situations

As a general statement, suicide is low in situations where families are close; when families are not close, suicide rates are high. Obviously, that statement is a generalization, but it points out the importance of close family ties.

Some suicide researchers believe that the family has the greatest impact of any other factor on influencing a child's suicidal thoughts, attempts, or actions. A child who grows up in a disorganized home marked by personality disturbances, alcoholism, or mental illness in parents becomes fragile and vulnerable — someone who may impulsively turn to self-destruction as a form of refuge.

Three of the nation's leading suicide researchers — Michael L. Peck, Norman L. Farberow, and Robert E. Litman — offer an excellent text, *Youth Suicide*, that examines various aspects of youth suicide. In case studies, Dr. Litman and Julie Diller identify three family "careers" that lead to suicide in teenagers:

1. Absent relationships — a family in which there is noninvolvement or isolation. The child is apt to be shy, withdrawn, and classified as a "misfit" or a "loner."

2. Negative relationships — destructive, violent interactions between parents and children that are usually characterized by physical abuse and interpersonal turmoil.

3. The "classical crisis case" — a family characterized by relatively "normal" relationships in which a person becomes suicidal in response to a sudden crisis, such as the loss of a family member.

In addition to the family "careers" identified by Litman and Diller, researchers have identified some specific family factors that may increase risk.

The Effects of Loss

Studies show that the risk of suicide increases among teenagers who have experienced the loss of a parent, a significant relative, or a guardian during their early life. In other cases, the "loss" may be the loss of an intact family unit as a result of death, divorce, separation, or a change in the family's status. In still other cases the "loss" may be the loss of a pet, the loss of the ability to fulfill a career aspiration, the loss of feeling a part of the group, or some other loss.

In some cases, especially among younger children and early adolescents, the suicide may be an attempt to join a loved one who has died.

Joshua had always had an intense and close relationship with his father; from the time Joshua was two years old, his father had become self-employed (first in sound recordings, then in real estate investments), while his mother had held down a traditional "away-from-home" employment role. While his mother worked twelve or fourteen hours a day at the advertising agency she founded, Joshua's father spent his hours at home; even when he had to leave for short periods of time to transact business or take care of other errands, he took Joshua with him. As Joshua became older, the two of them were often seen fishing in a nearby river, steering dirt bikes over the rolling foothills east of town, swimming at a nearby recreation center, or playing a vigorous game of football with a few of the neighborhood kids. Joshua loved his mother, but he formed his deepest attachment to his father.

When Joshua was eleven, his father was shot and killed as an innocent bystander in a drugstore robbery. Joshua was devastated by his father's death. His grades in school plummeted, and his ability to concentrate was shattered. He no longer ran through the field from school in an eager rush to get home; fingering the key to the front door in his pocket, he shuffled the long way, down the highway and along the asphalt roads of the neighborhood. As his key clicked in the lock, he

---

"There has been more and more invasion of the family from the outside. More and more pressures are making it very hard for parents to have positive relationships with their kids. There are so many divorces, so many immature people who are marrying and having children, so many kids who are being seduced by drugs and liquor that act as a low-level anesthesia that gives them an easy way out of any responsibility. But without a strong family structure, and positive models for emotional growth, we're not going to be raising people healthy enough to carry on."

—Dr. J.E. Geist, Adolescent Psychiatrist, Milwaukee

knew what waited on the other side of the door — not his father's enthusiastic reception, but the echoing silence of empty rooms.

Joshua's plight was deepened by his mother's difficulty in coping with the death. In an attempt to deal with her own depression and loneliness, she withdrew; instead of becoming a companion to her son, she closed him out. She would often retreat to her bedroom, lock her door, and leave Joshua in the family room, alone with a bowl of popcorn and the television set. Whenever he tried to seek comfort from her, she reacted in a frenzy of meaningless activity that helped her forget her own pain.

When school let out for the summer, the situation worsened. During the school year, Joshua had at least been kept busy for six hours a day in the confines of the classroom; now the entire day loomed ahead of him, empty and threatening. Joshua remembered last summer, when he and his dad had gone camping with a few of his friends, when they had formed a rough baseball diamond on a vacant lot down the street and his dad had always agreed to be the catcher. Joshua couldn't face a summer without his dad — he wanted to be where his father was. Joshua also wanted to die like his father had died; and one balmy afternoon he broke the glass on the gun cabinet in the basement (the one his mother had meant to sell), selected a handgun with a jeweled grip, and placed a bullet neatly and precisely through his head.

In other cases, the effect of a loss in the family inspires the desire to seek revenge.

Sixteen-year-old Kristen was understandably upset when, after almost twenty years of marriage, her parents decided to divorce. Kristen had always had a difficult time getting along with her mother — Kate was independent, stubborn, and critical — so Kristen believed beyond a doubt that the divorce was all her mother's fault. Her father was too kind and patient, Kristen reasoned; he probably couldn't stand living with Kate any longer.

In her rage over the breakup of her family and her desire to strike back at her mother for "causing" the family's problems,

Kristen hit upon a plan that she knew would cause her mother pain, embarrassment, and guilt: she would kill herself. Kristen carefully rehearsed the scene in her mind at least a hundred times — her mother would be devastated, would be worried about what the neighbors would think, would be plagued with guilt over failing her daughter. Each time she rehearsed the scene, she received delicious satisfaction from her mother's squirming and pain.

One night when her mother was scheduled to go out, Kristen decided to stage the scene she had so carefully rehearsed. She wedged a chair under her bedroom door, crawled under the coverlet on her bed, and washed a bottle of pain medication down her scratchy throat. As she waited under the coverlet for the medication to take effect, she could hear the distant voices of her brothers playing in the living room; she thought she could distinguish the animated conversation of her neighbors drifting up from the backyard next door. Maybe they were having a barbecue. Just as Kristen drifted from consciousness, a terrifying thought jolted her. She was getting back at her mother, but at a terrible price. Kristen hadn't really wanted to die — somehow, in her careful and thorough envisioning, she had left out this part. It hadn't really occurred to her. She struggled to throw back the coverlet, but the strength had left her arms. She died trying to get to the door to summon help.

The "Expendable Child" Dilemma

In what has been called the "expendable child" syndrome, a child believes that his parents want to be rid of him or wish him dead. For some reason, whether real or imagined, these adolescents feel they have "failed" the family or they feel that they are "to blame" for the family's problems. In a financially troubled family, for example, the teenager might feel responsible for the financial problems, mentally adding up the costs of new clothing, transportation to school, tuition at summer camp, and the fees for art class. A child might be the pawn over which divorcing parents battle, with the result that the child doesn't feel wanted by anyone. Or the teenager might feel that she has "failed" her family by getting poor grades, becoming pregnant, or getting into trouble with the law.

Becky had rebelled against her strict, religious parents for as long as she could remember. It seemed they were always finding fault with her — criticizing her friends, her clothing, her hairstyle, her music, or her sporadic efforts at school. When Becky met Rod, she was relieved to find someone who liked her and accepted her the way she was — no strings attached, no ivory-tower speeches on self-improvement. But she knew that her parents wouldn't accept Rod; in addition to his lack of religious conviction, he was Black — something Becky's parents wouldn't approve of.

Becky's reliance on Rod for affection deepened and became a substitute for the love she wished she could receive at home. Their intimacy increased in frequency, and one morning shortly after Christmas Becky learned she was pregnant.

At first, she was glad — this would teach her parents! As the days ticked by, however, she became first fearful of the discipline she would receive and then ashamed for the problems she would bring the family. Rod wasn't interested in marriage or in the responsibilities that come along with being a father; he deserted her almost immediately upon learning that she was pregnant. With only a few friends, her main network of support was her family. She yearned to tell them her plight, but held off in fear of the scene that was sure to follow. Her parents were outstanding, gifted, responsible members of the community; she was an embarrassment to them, a failure to the entire family. The rest of the family members were good, ambitious, productive, esteemed members of society; even her thirteen-

"The family seems to be a key element in preventing suicide. Loving, concerned parents and relatives are probably the best insurance."

—Dr. Michael Peck, Director of Youth Services,
  Suicide Prevention Center of Los Angeles

year-old sister had been recognized with a community service award for her volunteer work at the local hospital.

Once they learned her news, Becky knew that none of her family would want her around. She would be nothing but a disgrace, the black sheep in the family. Fearing abandonment and rejection by her family, she left her Volkswagen engine running in the closed garage, and peacefully drifted away.

Role Reversal

In a home troubled by role reversal, the parent is unable to emotionally handle the nurturing demands of being a parent; instead, the parent forces the child to do the nurturing. Even an adolescent who yearns to be independent and "in charge" ends up feeling resentful when a parent becomes dependent on him; pain, frustration, anxiety, and hostility often result. A teenager who is afraid to demonstrate those negative feelings — for fear of creating a crisis in the dependent parent — turns his feelings of hostility and frustration inward, and suicide may result.

When Brad's father moved out and remarried within a short time, Brad's mother began undergoing a severe emotional crisis. She turned her desperation on Brad, the oldest of her four children, and learned quickly to depend on him for comfort and emotional support. As she became increasingly more dependent, Brad became increasingly uncomfortable in his new

"Parents who divorce must set their rage aside when it comes to the kids. They should encourage contact by the children with both parents, and not set stumbling blocks in the way of unimpeded access to one parent. Children continue to need both parents, even if both parents no longer need each other."

—Melvin G. Goldzband, M.D., Clinical Professor of Psychiatry, University of California School of Medicine, San Diego

role with his mother.

At first, Brad tried to cope with the situation by spending less and less time at home, where his mother could manipulate and strangle him with her emotional demands. He began lingering at the gym after school, dribbling a worn basketball up and down the varnished basketball court, shooting repeated baskets through the fraying net. On weekends, he eagerly sought friends who would go with him to the mall or the movies — anything but spending time at home.

His mother reacted by imposing strict limits on Brad that kept him at home. His curfew was moved to an earlier slot, and she invented lists of chores that had to be done around the house on Saturdays. If Brad didn't comply, he was punished with a further reduction in privileges. Fearful that he would always be trapped in the emotionally draining relationship and unable to believe that his future would be better, he hanged himself in the bathroom one morning before his mother was awake.

Broken Homes

Approximately half of all those who successfully commit suicide come from a broken home, and approximately 65 percent of those who attempt suicide unsuccessfully also come from broken homes. There is an interesting difference, however: those who only attempt suicide tend to come from homes that have been disrupted by divorce, while those who successfully complete suicide tend to come from homes that have been broken by the death of a parent.

Pressure to Perform/Unrealistic Expectations

In a significant number of teenage suicides, the parents had placed a massive amount of pressure on the child to "measure up" to certain standards. While many — if not most — parents pressure their children to succeed, in the suicides it seemed that the parental pressure stemmed from the parent's own feelings of failure, insecurity, and inadequacy. The child learns quickly that the only way he can win approval from his parents is to "perform" in the desired channels.

A successful and busy attorney, Grant had largely neglected his duties as a father during the time his children were little; after all, he had reasoned, his wife was spending plenty of time with them and was capable of meeting their needs without his help. As Richard, the oldest of the three children, entered adolescence, Grant figured it was time to start being a real father.

Grant soon learned that it wasn't that easy — he had years of neglect to make up for. Richard seemed to be much more interested in his friends, television, and sports than he did in his father. Richard was understandably confused when his father suddenly started showering attention on him — attention aimed at his becoming an attorney. Grant started picking Richard up after school, driving him to the law office, having him do some simple clerking duties, and talking to him excitedly about having his own law practice someday. As long as Richard went along, his father was pleasant and easy to get along with; if Richard refused to go, saying that he wanted to shoot baskets with the guys after school or hang around with his friends at the mall, his father became sullen, angry, and depressed.

Richard caught on quickly: if he expected to enjoy a "happy" relationship with his father, he had to do what his father wanted him to do. Torn between his own ambition of being a chemical engineer and his desire to get along with his father, Richard swallowed his protests and accompanied his dad to the law firm. He even signed up for debate instead of taking the chemistry class he had been looking forward to throughout the ninth grade. He began to hate his father for it, and he began to resent the pressure he was under to become an attorney. He found it difficult to do well in debate, even though he was capable of doing the work, and he dreaded what would happen when his father saw his less-than-perfect grade. He didn't dare tell his father that he wasn't a member of the number-one debate team, either — and once he even paid his own way to a debate meet because he and his partner did not rank high enough to be invited to the meet.

As the pressure increased, so did Richard's hostility. Grant had become a task master, and Richard was panic-stricken at his supposed inability to meet his father's strict standards. At last he took the only way out that he knew: he downed a lethal potion that he mixed up in the school's chemistry lab.

Unfortunately, in many cases the parents' expectations of the child may not be nearly as great as what the child believes them to be. A teenager who is already beleaguered by self-criticism may imagine that her parents are holding out impossible standards for her to achieve. She may make incredible demands on herself, demands that her parents would never dream of making. Yet to her, the demands are coming from them, not from within herself.

In cases where parental expectation is real, tragedy can result. Pediatrician and director of the Adolescent Medical Unit at the University of California in San Francisco, Dr. Charles Irwin, says, "A lot of families expect that the minute youngsters become thirteen or fourteen, they should be capable of making it on their own. In reality, teenagers probably need as much support at that point in their lives as toddlers need, although of a different sort."

Psychotherapist Margery Fridstein, who works on Chicago's North Shore in an area that has been dubbed the nation's "suicide belt," says, "The parents put pressure on the child to either reproduce what they themselves have done, or do much

---

"Many troubled teenagers see death as an attractive alternative to stresses. For some, suicide is a way to find peace and escape, while for others it becomes a statement of protest and rage. As society becomes more violent, this is reflected in our children. We are seeing a dramatic increase in depression and self-destructive behavior among adolescents."

—*Dr. James Selkin, Past-President, American Association of Suicidology*

better. And the child may say, 'I can't, I can't, I'm going to give up.' "

Interestingly, however, the *absence* of pressure can be almost as devastating. Patricia Couto, executive director of the Crisis Intervention Center in Nashville, says, "In some way, there was more pressure on kids years ago. They were expected to go to school, grow intellectually, and be a doctor or a lawyer — and they got a lot of guidance. Now the expectations are still there, but the guidance is not. We tell the kids they must make their own decisions. It's a tremendous conflict, and I don't think teenagers are prepared to make decisions from all the choices they are given." Referring to her home of Nashville, she says, "This place is Music City, and the teenagers come in with their backpacks and guitars, and they think that they're going to walk right into the RCA Building and someone is going to hear them and they'll be a big hit. Well, the fact is they can't even get in the door, and in two days every cent they have is gone. A lot of them, boys and girls, wind up as prostitutes, and when they call us they say, 'I haven't eaten in three days, I have no place to stay.' " While Couto and her group are able to help most of them, tragedy is the result too often — in a recent year, twenty-two teenagers in Nashville committed suicide, and one was only eleven years old.

Lack of Communication and Understanding

Adolescents who are trying to work through the tasks confronting them need to talk about their feelings — and those who don't find an understanding listening ear at home can become discouraged and depressed. Sometimes the lack of communication is real; parents ignore or deny their child's feelings or react with hostility to a child's expressions of unhappiness or frustration. As a result, the child becomes isolated and starts to believe that something is dreadfully wrong with him. Unfortunately, some children imagine that their parents are responding — or will respond — with that kind of indifference or hostility. Thirteen-year-old Amanda tormented herself with depression and isolation instead of talking to her mother about her confusion because she was convinced that her mother would dismiss her or react with anger. In reality, her mother was aching to open up better lines of communication with Amanda. By the time her mother decided to take the risk of initiating the lines of communication, it was too late: burdened by self-hatred, self-criticism, fear, and isolation, Amanda jumped from the eighth-floor apartment balcony to the pebbled pavement below.

Alcoholism of a Parent

Almost one-fifth of the adolescents who attempt suicide come from homes where one or both parents have drinking problems. The suicides are probably not a reflection of the drinking problem itself, but instead of the problems that cause or accompany the drinking problem — the parent's own fear of failure, insecurity, low self-esteem, inability to communicate, poor parenting skills, and so on.

Suicide or Suicide Attempt of a Parent

Almost one-fourth of the adolescents who attempt or commit suicide have had a parent who has attempted or committed suicide. While suicide is not believed to be hereditary — in other words, it is not believed to be passed on from generation to generation in the genes — it can "run in families" for several reasons, as already discussed. A child learns most of his coping skills from his parents; a parent who is not able to cope with disappointment, frustration, or failure and who chooses to commit suicide in response to problems is teaching his or her child that suicide is the preferred way of coping when the going gets tough. In addition, the parent who commits suicide gives the child "permission" to do the same: if Mom did it, a sixteen-year-old may reason, then it is okay for me to do it, too.

When Mark was nine, his family was troubled by severe financial problems. His father's small accounting firm was failing, and it looked as though he stood to lose everything. On one warm spring day, just after the pussywillows had come out on the bushes that lined the fence and the forsythia blooms had become a bright profusion of yellow at the corner of the driveway, Mark's mother went to a conference for PTA presidents, leaving her husband in charge of the children for the day. Mark's father had seemed particularly upset, pacing back and forth in the kitchen for about an hour; finally, he told Mark, the oldest, "I'm going downstairs for a rest. Whatever you do, don't come downstairs. Just wait until Mommy gets home, and tell her that I'm down there."

Mark didn't think much about it, and he and the three younger children went outside to play. A few hours later when a man from the gas company came to read the meter, Mark ran downstairs to get his father. He was horrified by what he found: his father, a bluish-black color, was hanging from a steel rafter in the basement. His eyes bulged from his face with a vacant stare, and his tongue was so swollen that it completely filled his mouth.

Five years later, fourteen-year-old Mark was lonely and depressed: everyone else in the eighth grade seemed to have friends but him. He felt isolated and alone, and any attempts at making friends seemed to end in dismal failure. One early winter day as the sleet hammered against the windows, he reached the lowest point of depression he had yet encountered. Remembering his father's escape from his own problems, Mark crept down to the basement, looped his belt over the steel rafter, and joined his father in his despair.

Environmental Factors

Too often, our communities and schools have become "pressure cookers" for our teenagers, who are faced with a kind of stress that debilitates and cripples.

School Problems

A large percentage of those who attempt or commit suicide have above-average intelligence and IQs but are performing relatively poorly in school. Some teenagers who have committed suicide have been labeled as "learning problems" despite high potential and intelligence; some are reading several years behind their chronological development. Many are one to four years behind overall. Some students become anxious and discouraged over the inability to perform as they expect to in school.

The pressure to achieve academically can be particularly intense during adolescence, when the pressure is on to perform well enough for college acceptance. During elementary school and middle school, failure can be embarrassing and a reason for punishment at home; during the late years of junior high and high school, however, it can be the death knell for a potential career. A woman who is bound for medical school, for example, can see her hopes dashed and may be forced into choosing a different career if she doesn't consistently pull top grades — even in difficult subjects. With the heat on, some students set impossibly high standards for themselves and then view themselves as miserable, worthless failures if they fail to meet their own tough standards.

Sometimes the pressure comes from outside, too — failure in school is particularly painful to a teenager whose family places a great emphasis on academic achievement.

Darrin was a likeable thirteen-year-old who took great interest in sports of all kinds; he had been one of the most valuable players on his Little League baseball team, and he had been the only seventh-grader who made the track team. He saved up babysitting and paper route money and bought a mountain bike, and he and his friends loved to conquer the steep hills and the winding roads in the nearby canyon. It seemed that he was a natural athlete, and he loved being physically active.

Darrin wasn't a natural at academics, though. It seemed that he always had to work much harder than the other kids, even on simple problems. His friends breezed through their homework in forty-five minutes; Darrin chewed his pencils, wadded up paper, and finally finished with a wave of frustration in two hours. At first, he was able to keep up; later, when he lost his incentive and became involved in many other activities, he started to slip behind. By the middle of the school year, three of his teachers called his parents in for a conference.

"Darrin has plenty of ability," one of them told Darrin's father, a university professor. "He simply doesn't apply himself." She obviously hadn't seen him at his desk in his bedroom, working harder than any of his friends for what he *did* accomplish.

Darrin's parents — both university educated and close to the academic community — put the pressure on: if his grades didn't go up one full grade in each of his classes by the end of the year, he would not be allowed to go to the summer track camp in June. Darrin began working harder than he had ever worked; his bike, dusty from misuse, sat propped against the side of the garage day after day while he struggled to do better on his homework. But, despite his efforts, things didn't improve too much; he just couldn't seem to do it. He felt miserable — not only would he miss the summer track camp, but he had failed his parents. They would be so ashamed. And he had failed himself. One chilly May afternoon, two weeks before school ended and grades were scheduled to come out, Darrin hopped on his dirt bike, sped up the canyon, and flung himself off a sheer cliff onto the jagged rocks below.

Religious Conflict

Most children prescribe to their parents' religion or their parents' religious values; adolescence is a time during which many children choose to move away from their parents' religion or religious values toward their own. That transition process generally takes some time — often years — and can leave a person effectively without a religious value system while the transition is being made. In a period marked by lack of religious values, a teenager is vulnerable and isolated; if he becomes stressed during such a period of vulnerability and isolation, tragedy can result.

Social Problems

Next to the family in importance to adolescents is the peer group. During adolescence, when major physical, social, and psychological changes are occurring, the pressures and inducements to test new behaviors, to rebel, and to identify with other people of similar ages going through similar experiences may be particularly compelling.

Social Loss

Adolescent suicide is often precipitated by the loss or threatened loss of a girlfriend or boyfriend or the loss of a "best" friend. Many suicidal adolescents have been characterized as lonely, rejected, withdrawn, isolated, and alienated; many have histories of stormy interpersonal relationships and problems in sustaining friendships. Most cannot tolerate being alone.

For teenagers who have a difficult time maintaining relationships, the threatened or perceived loss of a friend or romantic partner can be too much to withstand.

Stephanie had always been shy and overweight; her poor self-image made her seem gloomy and uninteresting to the other kids her age, and she did not have many friends among the other ninth-graders at the school. On the few occasions when she had succeeded in making a friend, she had smothered her with demands and emotional dependency. She had gained a reputation as someone who could only have one friend at a time, and most of the kids steered clear.

Stephanie played the violin in the school orchestra, and finally succeeded in growing close to a tenth-grader who also played the violin and who shared her music stand in orchestra class. The two became fast friends, spending hours with each other during and after school. Everything was fine until Maria, the other violinist, tried to include a viola player in the friendship. Stephanie became threatening and demanding. One day she slipped Maria a hastily scrawled note accusing her of betrayal and desertion.

Maria acted with startled disbelief. *If I go ahead and befriend*

Irene, she reasoned, Stephanie will relax and join in. But Stephanie didn't. While Maria's circle of friends increased quite rapidly, Stephanie remained isolated and withdrawn. She saw what happened as a loss of her "only" friend, and she couldn't bear the loneliness and betrayal. She swallowed seventy-five aspirin after leaving another disturbing note inside Maria's violin case.

Social Isolation

Almost three-fourths of those who attempt suicide have little or no social contact with others their own age; they are in every sense of the word, "loners." At a time when the peer group is so important, social isolation can be devastating. Loners, says psychologist Linda Share, "are the ones who actually kill themselves. They're the ones who aren't recognized by the teachers because they never say a word, and none of the classmates knows who they are because they're so nondescript. Often, in going back to the people who surrounded the victim to find out what led up to the suicide (a process known as an 'emotional autopsy'), they have a hard time remembering who the teenager was."

Many loners have been that way all of their lives — most have a long history of spending all their spare time alone instead of on the swing set with the neighbors or playing dolls under the

---

"These loners are the ones who actually kill themselves. They're the ones who aren't recognized by the teachers because they never say a word, and none of the classmates knows who they are because they're so nondescript. Often, in going back to the people who surrounded the victim to find out what led up to the suicide, they have a hard time remembering who the teenager was."

—Linda Share, Crossroads Hospital, Van Nuys, California

elm tree. Many have poor relationships with adults as well as those their own age; when they do make friends, the relationship is likely to be shallow and superficial. (Friends who are asked about the loner tend to respond, "Well, I didn't really know him all that well.")

Most loners come from intact families headed by relatively "normal" parents, but many come from families in which parents themselves have a poor self-image. Such parents often misinterpret the child's complaints or unhappiness as a direct statement about their own poor parenting. As a result, they become defensive and compensatory: they go to great lengths to convince the teenager that he is not really unhappy. Such a child realizes early that what he thinks of himself and what his parents think of him is entirely different, he stops communicating his feelings to his parents (and, eventually, he stops communicating them to others).

The loner is one of the highest risks for suicide. Why? Other teenagers will give plenty of clues (verbal and otherwise) about the impending suicide, allowing for rescue by concerned friends and family members. The loner, who has been conditioned to avoid expressing his feelings, often does not give a clue as to his desperate state. He quietly becomes so terrified and overwhelmed by his feelings of despair or helplessness that he kills himself without letting on to anyone else.

Jackie had always been a quiet child; while the other children in the neighborhood chased up and down the sloping sidewalk on roller skates or climbed the towering maple tree in the front yard, she spent her time alone. Her mother often found her in a corner of her room, scribbling methodically in a coloring book or reading a musty library book. But she was intelligent and a good student, so her parents didn't worry excessively about her.

She never seemed to have close friends — or any friends, for that matter — but she didn't complain much about being lonely. Her parents assumed that she was simply a quiet student who had different interests than the other girls her age. When she entered high school and the other girls started dating, Jackie didn't. Her parents tried to compensate by buying her stylish clothes, decorating her room, and taking her on vacations. They were shocked one Thursday night to discover her body on the cold tile floor of the bathroom, a bullet through her head. It was two days before the junior prom, and her isolation had reached its chilling climax.

Sexual Maladjustment

As discussed, adolescence is a time of burgeoning sexual development — a time when a teenager feels as though he is a display on center stage as he watches his body change and develop. When something in that development goes awry (whether real or imagined), a teenager's entire self-concept and image can be shattered. Suicide has been known to result from conflicts associated with homosexuality; stifling sexual inhibition or terror associated with sexuality; pregnancy; confusion over sexual identity; guilt over sexual activity; promiscuity; sexual assault by a parent; or the use of sex in exchange for closeness or friendship.

Oddly, there is a tendency among those who commit suicide to have had less sexual experience than other teenagers in the same age group. The lack of sexual experience may be an indication of emotional immaturity, social isolation, social alienation, conflicts at home, or other factors known to contribute to suicide.

Mason, a precocious fourteen-year-old, had never really been interested in girls; during his friends' animated locker room discussions of their latest conquests he maintained a passive disinterest in the lurid details that had most of the boys captive. Although he had never had a homosexual experience, he was disturbed to find himself fantasizing about one boy who shared his gym locker. He didn't dare mention his fantasies to anyone, especially his parents; instead, he kept them bottled up, worried that he was abnormal. Mason's fears increased when a physician came to talk to the eighth-grade assembly; when a student asked about homosexuality, the doctor launched off on a frightening discourse about psychiatric disturbance and deep-seated problems.

Mason's problems reached a height one sultry July afternoon when he and four of his friends went to the high school baseball field to watch a championship playoff. Sometime during the sixth inning, Mason wandered away from the group and toward the temporary restrooms that had been constructed at the edge of the field for the tournament crowds. As he shuffled toward one of the shelters, he saw a tall, dark-haired boy of about eighteen behind a set of abandoned bleachers. The boy signaled to him, beckoning him to come closer. A quick conversation followed, and Mason had his first experience behind the bleachers. It was quick, intense, and extremely exciting for Mason. As he went back toward his friends, who were then sipping icy Cokes, he was flooded with conflicting emotions. He was excited by the experience, relieved to find that his fantasies had been founded in some truth, overwhelmed by guilt at what he had done, and consumed by worry over his "abnormality."

His friends noticed that he was quiet and withdrawn through the remainder of the game, but they didn't think it was anything serious. They were shocked to hear the next morning that he had shot himself through the neck with his father's hunting rifle.

Social Alienation

An adolescent who is socially isolated has usually partly chosen that isolation through a long history of preferring to be alone, spending his spare time alone, and so on. A teenager who is a victim of social alienation is one who has suffered the crushing rejection after making an attempt to be accepted. Once rejected or alienated, the teenager becomes isolated, powerless, helpless, and uncommunicative; most significant interpersonal relationships break down. In such a condition of isolation and loneliness, he is a primary risk for suicide.

Kent had been an active, enthusiastic, bright teenager until his critical injuries in an automobile accident; when he was pinned beneath the wrecked and twisted frame of a friend's car, the fire that followed charred the skin on both arms and literally melted the skin on his face into a shapeless, charred mass. Physicians at the hospital had done everything possible to reconstruct his face, but the mass of scar tissue pulled his nose into a contorted shape, fused the corners of his mouth together, and webbed one eye closed. Subsequent surgeries were successful in opening the eye, but the mass of scar tissue remained.

Kent was, plain and simple, horrifying to look at. His friends at the small rural high school were uncomfortable gazing at him; they found excuses to avoid him and invented ways to exclude him from their activities. Once sought-after for his disarming good looks, he was now sentenced like a leper.

One February afternoon he was feeling particularly alone and discouraged. Spotting a group of friends at a table in the school lunchroom, he steered in their direction; they were excitedly discussing the upcoming game against a rival school, gesturing wildly. As Kent approached and took a seat at the end of the table, the others fell silent; one by one, and in rapid succession, they dabbed at the corners of their mouths with the shredded napkins and thrust their trays onto the conveyor belt, leaving the lunchroom. Kent remained alone at the table, staring into his food. As soon as he got home from school he removed his favorite hunting knife from its tooled leather sheath, wandered into the alfalfa fields behind his home, and carved two deep incisions through his wrists. As the blood spurted with force from the wounds, he made one last deep slash — across the scar tissue on his face.

The importance of relationships cannot be emphasized too much. "Tender loving care," social supports, networking, or whatever you want to call it has now been recognized by medical science as a powerful healing force. As early as the eighteenth century, researchers struggled to assign some kind of scientific explanation to the powerful influence that encouragement, caring, and intimacy have on healing.

Good social networking — high involvement with other people — is a healing force that can keep you young, healthy, and protected from the loneliness and isolation that can lead to suicidal depression. Alfred N. Larsen, national director of the

Retired Senior Volunteer Program (RSVP), sees more than a quarter of a million elderly people placed in community volunteer jobs each year. While many elderly people lose family members, lose friends, become ill, and generally lose a purpose in life, those involved in RSVP generally enjoy better health and make fewer visits to the doctor.

Some researchers believe that good social networking is an instinct — that even in times of disaster or crisis, we reach out to others as a way of gaining strength ourselves. One researcher, who pored over the data on more than a hundred natural disasters, discovered a strong pattern of people helping other people — even when their own lives were disrupted, they almost invariably reached out to help others. That reaching out, the researcher believes, was the healing force that enabled all to survive. Numerous studies have been done that also demonstrate that where emotional support was a component of presurgery care in hospitalized children and adults, patients fared better, required less anesthesia, and required fewer days of hospitalization.

Social relationships can also help ease the effects of stress in two ways: in the face of solid social relationships, the amount of stress is reduced and the person's ability to cope with stress is increased. The net effect of stress is modified and well-being is enhanced. Studies show that social support reduces the likelihood of psychological and physical symptoms — such as anxiety, depression, and dizziness — during stress. Close family and social relationships in particular help contribute to self-confidence and a sense of security in dealing with the demands of daily living.

The available evidence in animals and humans suggests that high levels of social support may play a stress-buffering role and to some degree protect an individual from the effects of cumulative life changes. In fact, Dr. Irwin Sarason and his colleagues at the University of Washington suggest that there are data consistent with the view that adults who are self-reliant, adept at coping with stress, and able to maintain a task-oriented attitude in the face of challenges frequently had childhoods marked by the personal security that goes along with warm relationships and shared experiences and responsibilities.

What happens when a person's network of social relationships is seriously deficient? Loneliness occurs. Social alienation creeps in. It's a painful warning signal that a person's social relations are suffering in some important way — either in quantity or in quality. The person's actual social relations don't match up to his needs: and because a person's needs may include things such as close emotional ties or someone in whom to trust, a person can very definitely be "lonely in a crowd."

According to researchers at the United States Department of Health and Human Services, many lonely people have certain distinctive social behaviors that make it difficult for them to form and/or maintain relationships. They may be extremely shy, for example, and may find it very difficult to introduce themselves, participate in groups, enjoy parties, make phone calls to initiate social activities, and so on. They may suffer from a crippling lack of self-esteem, or may be excrutiatingly self-conscious. Many lonely people are introverted, are not able to be assertive, and feel that they are controlled by others.

Lonely people also tend to have distinct patterns of interaction. When they are having a conversation with someone else, they respond slowly to the other person's statements, change the subject often, talk more about themselves, and ask few questions of the other person. A researcher who studied these patterns says that lonely people are "self-focused and nonresponsive."

Lonely people also often had problems relating to their parents. Many lonely people say that their parents did not give emotional nurturance, that they failed to give guidance or support, and that they did not encourage their children to strive for relationships or popularity. Many lonely people remember their parents as remote, not trustworthy, and disagreeable.

No one is immune from loneliness and social isolation or alienation. Some people are at higher risk — and teenagers are among those at risk. Why? Adolescents usually have more opportunity for social interaction, but they often fail; they have unrealistic expectations about what friendships should involve. As a result, their needs are not met.

Increasing Mobility

As few as two or three decades ago, there was little mobility in our society. People married, bought a house, retired from their first job, and spent their retirement years in the house they had bought as newlyweds. The maple tree they planted as a seedling grew to tower above the roof, providing cooling shade from the searing August sun, and all the neighbors grew old together.

Today we live in a highly mobile society. In some professions it is ordinary and expected to change jobs every three or four years; families often live in four or five houses before settling on the "dream home." Corporate executives are transferred every few years by the company, and families pull up stakes as an ordinary and expected part of life.

The moving vans rumbling down quiet suburban streets and the "For Sale" signs dotting the well-manicured lawns in most subdivisions have brought about a crisis for some adolescents: faced with the stress of making new friends in a new location, some teenagers find they become lonely, withdrawn, and isolated. Instead of being the vehicle for new opportunities, the mobility becomes a source of agony and depression.

The Media/Suggestibility

While significant studies have not borne out the theory, many researchers feel that media discussion of suicide, newspaper reports of suicides, and suicides shown in the movies and on television may promote suggestibility among teenagers who are suicide-prone. Friends and relatives of Robbie DeLaValliere, the first of the Westchester County cluster suicides, are convinced that his hanging was an imitation of the Naval cadet's self-destruction in *An Officer and A Gentleman*, which Robbie had seen only weeks before his death.

Some researchers who are studying the recent "cluster suicides" believe that media attention given to a suicide may bring an adolescent's own crisis to the surface. Seeing that another troubled teenager has "escaped," ended his problems, or put an end to his pain may give the teenager the courage or the incentive to do the same. In some cluster suicides, the method is limited — all the adolescents in a single town may die by hanging, for example, which is how the first teenager killed himself. In other cases of cluster suicides, adolescents may mimic aspects of the suicide that they read about in newspapers or see on the evening news (such as leaving a note pinned to the adolescent's shirt).

Much as in the situation of the family suicide, the suicide of another adolescent that is publicized tends to give other teenagers "permission" to do the same.

Romanticized Attitude Toward Suicide

All of us remember the tragic tale of Romeo and Juliet, the star-crossed lovers who were prevented from marrying because of an ages-old feud between their families and who sealed their love by their double suicide. It was all very romantic, that tale of the Montagues and the Capulets, and we agonized over the vision of the two of them perishing, unfulfilled.

Unfortunately, some adolescents hold that kind of romanticized vision of their own suicide. Rationally, we know death to be irreversible, final, and a complete cessation of all bodily functions; these teenagers, however, see death emotionally as a temporary way of escaping a painful and troubled existence. In their minds, they see death as a kind, gentle, nurturing experience that will soothe and heal; somehow, they expect to return from that gentle experience, warmed and strengthened to face their problems with new strength. They *know* that death is final, but they view suicide romantically, emotionally, and irrationally. Many who attempt suicide later reveal that they didn't actually intend to die — they hadn't realized that they might actually cease to exist.

This kind of a romanticized look at suicide occurs more frequently in cases of "cluster suicides," especially when suicide is committed or attempted by an adolescent who is popular, renowned for his athletic skill, accomplished in some area (such as debate or drama), or well-known and well-respected by the other teenagers in the school or town. Suicide then becomes "accepted," an approved way of coping or dealing with problems.

Alcohol/Drug Use

As mentioned, suicide rates are higher among adolescents who frequently use alcohol and/or drugs. The fact that the teenager uses drugs to begin with indicates a low impulse control and a low threshhold for frustration and boredom. Those personality traits — not the drug use itself — may explain the higher rate among adolescent drug users.

But there's another reason why drug and alcohol use may lead to higher rates of suicide: substance abuse lowers a teenager's resistance and coping ability, leaving him vulnerable to stress and upsetting emotions. Those who are addicted run the highest risk of all.

Feelings of Powerlessness

Teenagers are like all of the rest of us: they like to feel reasonably competent in social situations. When something happens that makes a teenager feel powerless over the things that are happening around him (as often occurs during adolescence), his tendency toward suicidal thought or action increases.

Powerlessness brings with it a terrifying feeling of losing control — a chronic state of helplessness and vulnerability that is particularly disturbing to an adolescent who has begun to value his ability to be independent and emancipated from his parents. Suddenly his world starts to crumble — he's not nearly as capable as he thought he was, and he is faced with losing his hard-won independence. Such a teenager, forced back into his parents' arms, may then begin to view his parents with hostility and resentment.

Powerlessness may stem from emotional problems, or it may originate from a physical illness or something else that is out of the adolescent's control.

Greg had always been an energetic, well-liked young man who participated in athletics and did well academically. He seemed to coast through his adolescence with less trauma than many and was eager to begin his senior year at high school.

In the middle of July while his family was vacationing at Disneyland, Greg developed severe abdominal pains. At first, his parents suspected intestinal flu; but when the pains came and went without logical cause, they began to get worried. As soon as they returned to their Wyoming home, they took Greg to see the family doctor. After referrals to a series of specialists, Greg was diagnosed as having ileocolitis — a chronic disease of the intestine characterized by intense pain, occasional bleeding, weight loss, anemia, and arthritis. Doctors advised him to stay out of school for at least a semester — preferably a year — and to undergo intensive medical treatment aimed at improving his condition.

The next few months became a blur of weekly outpatient testing and treatment, frequent but brief hospitalization, and bottles of medication lined up on the medicine cabinet shelf. His one refuge became his room at home — a wonderland he had filled with the rare books he loved to collect, intricate ship models, and photographs from the post-Civil War period.

One morning while he and his mother were at the clinic for tests, a fire attributed to an electrical short in the kitchen swept rapidly through the house, engulfing Greg's room and consuming the books, photographs, and models he had so painstakingly arranged on the shelves around his bed. When Greg and his mother returned home, he was frantic over the loss. He had been totally dependent on his parents and his doctors for months; now it seemed as if he didn't have control over anything at all.

That evening, desperate to gain some control over *something*, he took a handful of the codeine pills the doctor had prescribed for pain; he did not die, and his doctors and parents convinced themselves that it was an accidental overdose brought on by confusion over the fire and the temporary dislocation to a neighbor's home. Two months later, when Greg's family finally moved back into their own home, he located one of his father's guns and shot himself in the chest.

Depression

Depression is now considered to be the most common factor leading to adolescent suicide — and, startingly, some experts estimate that as many as half of all teenagers suffer from depression in varying degrees of severity.

What is depression? The major symptom of depression, according to the American Psychiatric Association, is a fairly prominent and persistent loss of pleasure in and interest in usual activities and pursuits. Feelings of sadness, hopelessness, and discouragement pervade the depressed individual.

According to information published by the National Institute of Mental Health, the term "depression" can be used to refer to several related but distinct conditions. Depression can refer to a mood that all of us experience at one time or another in response to disappointments, frustrations, and sorrows. It is part of the normal ups and downs of normal life. Depression can also refer to symptoms of sadness, loss of energy, inability to experience pleasure, feelings of helplessness, and bodily complaints that may be short-lived but that are beyond what we

"It is obvious that depression — and its dark angels, isolation, helplessness, hopelessness — can ultimately lead to thoughts of suicide. But most people experience these emotions from time to time and learn to control them. The difficult thing is to find ways of helping young people deal with frustration and depression that even adults at times cannot manage."

—John Langone, *"Too Weary to Go On,"* Discover

normally experience in response to disappointment or frustration.

Then there is clinical depression. It's the kind of depression that is characterized by depressed mood with associated features, persistence over time, and some impairment of functioning. Someone who is clinically depressed may suffer appetite and sleep disturbances, loss of energy, feelings of pessimism, hopelessness, the inability to experience pleasure, and thoughts of death and suicide. At its best, clinical depression lasts for a few weeks; at its worst, it may persist for years. It is the kind of depression that leads to suicide.

As discussed, the process of adolescence is conflicting, complicated, and demanding. Adolescents undergo a shakeup physically, psychologically, emotionally, and socially. There are pressures from within (involving hormonal changes, bodily changes, and the awakening of sexual desire) as well as from without (involving the need for social approval, meaningful relationships, acceptance, academic performance, and pressure to succeed). It is a time of adaptation and integration into the broader society and a time of achieving separation from the family. It is a time of complicated conflicts and the need to establish a distinct identity.

It is also a time when a person is susceptible to deep depression. Why? Some of the factors identified by the National

---

"Adolescents with so-called masked depression don't necessarily look or seem sad but they engage in certain activities to escape from their sad thoughts. Antisocial behavior may appear. They may start to drink or use drugs, fight, commit acts of vandalism, run away from home, or become sexually promiscuous. They may do all sorts of things they've never even considered before. But those manifest symptoms are a defense against the painful and unacceptable depressive affect."

—Dr. Iris Litt, Director, Adolescent Medicine,
Stanford University School of Medicine

Institute of Mental Health include the following:

Many adolescents suffer low self-esteem. One of the greatest determinants of depression is low self-esteem. Self-esteem, as defined by the National Institute of Mental Health, is a judgment or estimate of your own value or worth — the extent to which you feel capable, significant, successful, and worthy.

High self-esteem, or a positive estimate of your own worth, is characterized by self-confidence, independence, assertiveness, self-respect, pride, self-acceptance, expressiveness, and dominance. Low self-esteem, or a negative estimate of your own worth, is characterized by obedience, passivity, helplessness, inferiority, powerlessness, timidity, self-rejection, self-hatred, conformity, self-doubting, submissiveness, unworthiness, and self-punishment.

There are four basic sources of self-esteem: *power*, or the ability to influence and control others; *significance*, marked by the acceptance, attention, and affection of others; *virtue*, measured by adherence to moral and ethical standards; and *competence*, or the successful performance in meeting the demands for achievement. High self-esteem does not depend on success in all four sources; for example, you may have high self-esteem through being highly competent without being virtuous, significant, or powerful.

One of the greatest indicators of depression is low self-esteem — a negative concept associated with self-reproach and self-blame, self-dislike, and self-criticism. An adolescent's feelings of self-reproach and criticism may range from mild to extreme. In a mild state, an adolescent may think, "I've let everybody down . . . if only I had tried harder, I could have made the grade." In an extreme, the adolescent may think, "I'm despicable, I'm worthless, I hate myself."

A depressed adolescent looks at himself as lacking such attributes as ability, performance, intelligence, health, strength, personal attraction, popularity, or financial resources. In a mild form, the teenager may have an excessive reaction to errors or difficulties, with a tendency to see such errors as grounded in a defect or deficiency within himself. He may criticize himself for failing to live up to his own rigid standards of perfection, and he may be unable to accept the notion that "to err is human."

In its severe form, adolescent depression brings a severe downgrading of self. The adolescent becomes convinced that she is totally worthless, inept, inadequate, and impoverished — she believes that she is a total failure and a burden to those around her. She sees herself as an object of public disapproval, like a social leper or a criminal. She may think something like, "I am responsible for everything bad in the world. There's no way I can be punished enough for my sins. I wish you would take me out and hang me."

It is difficult to imagine a teenager feeling such despair, but it *does* happen — in fact, we are now recognizing that deep clinical depression even happens in children as young as two or three years of age. Experts now believe that the number of suicides could be dramatically decreased if we properly recognized the signs of depression and took aggressive action to help children and adolescents who suffer from it. *(The specific signs and symptoms of depression will be listed in the chapter titled "Warning Signs and Symptoms of Suicidal Adolescents.")*

Strong peer attachment. Depression may result when a teenager becomes firmly attached to his peers to the exclusion of any emotional bonds with his parents. Isolation from peers can also lead to debilitating depression as a teenager struggles with social withdrawal or alienation. Those who are least likely to suffer from depression are the adolescents who have been able to strike a healthy balance: they have a strong attachment to their parents and a firm relationship with their peers.

"Is it possible that young people, growing up in communities in which the satisfactions that most people have to strive for are readily available, are deprived of some of the challenges that are essential to maturity?"

—*George S. Hendry, Professor of Theology, Princeton University*

Child-rearing style of the parent. Depression often results when parents adopt a "laissez-faire" attitude toward discipline: they separate themselves from the child, refusing to intervene or interfere. Such parents refuse to set limits, and the teenager becomes confused and upset. Depression also results commonly from homes where parents are authoritarian, demanding unquestioned obedience from children. An adolescent growing up in such a home is not allowed to go the normal questioning process that allows him to formulate his own ideals, values, and morals and that allows a healthy separation from the total dependence on his parents.

The lowest risk of depression stems from homes where adolescents are reared in a democratic atmosphere: parents set up rules and guidelines but encourage participation and discussion among all family members. A teenager in such a family receives guidance and help but is allowed to make the gradual transition into adulthood.

Depressed parents. Parents who are depressed themselves tend to rear children who suffer from deep clinical depression that impairs their ability to function.

Adolescent girls tend to suffer consistently higher levels of depression than boys, especially as adolescence progresses. The same percentages of boys and girls suffer from depression at about age thirteen, but the gap widens substantially between the ages of fourteen and eighteen. Recently, however, researchers have theorized an interesting distinction: adolescent boys who are depressed have a much higher tendency toward delinquent behavior; delinquent behavior in adolescent boys, then, might be the equivalent of depression in adolescent girls.

Developmental Factors

Involvement in Cults

While involvement in cults does not usually lead directly to suicide (except in the few well-known cases, such as that of the Reverend Jim Jones), involvement in cults can lead to personality factors that may place adolescents at risk. According to Dr. Saul Levine, professor of psychiatry at the University of Toronto Medical School, cult involvement can result in the following personality developments:

—Adolescents feel estranged in society, and so they join a "group" (cult) in which they can feel a part, feel a sense of belonging. Children who did not feel needed by their parents at home suddenly feel a surge of importance within their new group. Many were not required to work at home, and few — if any — were economic necessities to their parents. In the cult, however, they must "work" for the economic well-being of the group. They are an essential part of the whole.

It's not genuine, though. As Dr. Levine says, "One is struck by a certain juvenile quality in much of the work required of cult group members. Selling flowers reminds one of raising money for the sixth grade's annual trip to Washington, D.C., or selling cookies for the Scouts. There is a sort of playing at being grown up."

And, Levine points out, the real business of most of the cults goes on way above the heads of most cult members.

—Adolescents remove themselves from the stability of a family unit to the pseudo-family of a cult. Cult members become like children; they are stripped of power and

---

"Before joining a cult, what strikes these young men and women as fateful decisions — what 'style' of person to be, what career to prepare for — have weighed them down. After joining, these concerns evaporate. The single decision to join may be momentous, but it is the only choice the joiner has to make."

—Saul Levine, M.D., Professor of Psychiatry, University of Toronto Medical School

possessions. They may not completely understand the teachings of their elders. Still, they find comfort in finding that there are people "above" who can answer any question and solve any problem.

—They lose individual identity. They become part of the group, and are identified (even to themselves) as a segment of the group unit. They wear the same clothes, share the same beliefs, eat the same food, work for the same cause, and do the same things. They lose the essential quality of learning to depend on themselves, of developing their own strength with which to face problems.

—They are not forced to deal with impulses that may have frightened them. Adolescence is a period of burgeoning development, and some of the impulses that go along with that development can be difficult and frightening. But strength comes through facing those impulses and learning to control them. In a cult, the adolescent is stripped of all responsibility. There is no need to cope with the impulses; there is no opportunity to develop strength.

—Most adolescents join a cult at a crossroads: at a junction in life when they had to make a big decision or enter a new phase of their lives. Instead of having to face the decision and learn to make decisions (an important part of learning to cope), the teenager no longer has to make the decision. The only decision he has to make is to join the cult; after that, his decisions are all made for him. He is part of the group, part of the unit. He thinks and eats and behaves and does what he is told.

Loneliness

Strong indication suggests that adolescents experience more loneliness than people in any other age group. Teenagers as young as twelve may begin to suffer debilitating loneliness, and it may persist until an adolescent is sixteen or eighteen.

According to the National Institute of Mental Health, the

position of the adolescent in today's society apparently contributes to a sense of loneliness, meaninglessness, powerlessness, and isolation. There is a role ambiguity in that adolescents are neither children nor adults. School failure can create a strong sense of rejection; lack of meaning and challenge can create boredom and apathy; social expectations may be unrealistic; and strong forces may oppose the struggle for independence and autonomy.

In one study (Brennan) reported by the National Institute of Mental Health, loneliness is seen broadly as a response to some perceived or vaguely experienced deficit in relationships. The major forms of loneliness are emotional isolation, social isolation, spiritual loneliness, and existential loneliness.

Emotional isolation results from a lack of close, intimate relating and stems from a loss of attachment figures. Associated feelings include a sense of emptiness, loss, unfulfillment, anger, and unhappiness.

Social isolation results from a lack of social connectedness or integration with peers or the community. Associated feelings include boredom, a sense of being on the outside and not belonging anywhere, and a desire to find new friends and move to new places.

Along with loneliness come feelings of estrangement. According to a study conducted by the Education Commission of the States, the increasing suicide rate is a sign of "alienation and disconnection." The alienation and disconnection, say authors of the report, "suggest that family, community, school, and other agencies of socialization and integration are not working as they once were."

"Across the nation, growing numbers of young people from comfortable homes are being labeled 'runaways,' 'push-outs,' or 'bag kids.'

—*U.S. News & World Report*

Disturbing statistics from the report show that approximately 2.4 million sixteen- to nineteen-year-olds (or about 15 percent of that population) are already "disconnected" from society as a result of drug abuse, delinquency, pregnancy, unemployment, and dropping out of school. The implications, say study authors, are even more disturbing: those 2.4 million teenagers who are "disconnected" are unlikely to become productive adults.

Spiritual loneliness emerges from a lack of meaning or significance in one's life. Associated feelings include boredom, aimlessness, emptiness, despair, hollowness, distractability, daydreaming, a feeling of being unchallenged and not using one's potential — or, alternately, rebellion, anger, frustration, and blaming.

Existential loneliness results from an awareness of the basic human condition of separateness, mortality, death, finiteness,

"At least 15 percent of all American teenagers between the ages of 16 and 19 are unlikely to become productive adults because they already are 'disconnected' from society as a result of drug abuse, delinquency, pregnancy, unemployment and dropping out of school. We are talking about, by conservative estimate, 1,250,000 white, 750,000 black, and 375,000 Hispanic 16- to 19-year-olds at risk. Drug and alcohol abuse among young people is up 60-fold since 1960. Teenage pregnancy is up 109 percent among whites and 10 percent among non-whites since 1960. A million teens become pregnant each year. Teenage homicide is up 'an astounding 232 percent for whites' and 16 percent for nonwhites since 1950, while suicide is up more than 200 percent since 1950. A teenager commits suicide every 90 minutes. The higher incidences of suicide, crime, drug use, and pregnancy among teens are all signs of alienation and disconnection."

—Education Commission of the States

and responsibility in one's life. Associated feelings include a sense of fear, dread, anguish, and terror.

The adolescent is confronted with considerable developmental changes in relationship with others. There is a necessary adjustment to losses or breaking off of critical attachments and the surfacing of new needs and desires for relations with others. Some of the significant developmental changes that can increase loneliness and lead to suicidal feelings include:

—A loss of childhood identity and psychological social reference points, resulting in a sense of uncertainty and confusion, as well as an increased need for self-understanding and reassurance and guidance from others.

—A loss of the attachment bond to parents, which can be critical and lead to emotional isolation.

—An increased awareness of separateness. Cognitive development in adolescence produces an increased awareness of "separateness" and mortality.

—New needs for heterosexual relationships derived from physiological and emotional maturing. The confidence and skills necessary to establish new relations may not be fully developed.

The characteristics of adolescents having high levels of loneliness include low self-esteem, marked by feelings of worthlessness, unattractiveness, unpopularity, and stupidity; feelings of powerlessness; passivity in structuring leisure-time activities; shyness and fear of risk-taking; selfishness; and lack of interest in others.

Suicide is only one of the inappropriate or destructive ways that adolescents often use to cope with loneliness. Other destructive methods of coping with pervasive loneliness include:

—Hero or heroine worship of celebrities; because the hero or heroine is not actually present and a vital part of the relationship, loneliness can be increased instead of decreased.

—Decreasing one's level of desire for relationships; if successful in this strategy, an adolescent could permanently inhibit the healthy desire for deep interpersonal relationships, sentencing himself to a life of loneliness and isolation.

—Denying that loneliness exists; such denial may lead to impaired development and strangulation of feelings and emotions.

—Alternative forms of escape, such as drugs and alcohol; unfortunately, these often bring on new, more serious problems and can lead to deeper levels of despair. In the extreme, reliance on drugs and alcohol to soothe loneliness can lead to erosion of the sense of self.

Other Factors That Lead To Youth Suicide

While the major factors leading to adolescent suicide seem to center around depression, loneliness, shattered self-esteem, social isolation or alienation, pressure to perform, and problems within the family, there are a number of miscellaneous causes

---

"What we are seeing now is an epidemic of suicidal communication among young people. It is a way of saying, 'Someone help me.' Youth are desperate, unhappy, confused, and compulsive. They can't think of any other way out."

—*Michael Peck, Los Angeles Psychologist and Director, Youth Services and the Outpatient Clinic, Los Angeles Suicide Prevention Center*

that have been identified. Among the most common are the following:

Presence of Physical, Emotional, or Sexual Abuse in the Home

Sexual abuse is particularly at fault, but with any kind of abuse, the adolescent may see suicide as the only way out of the situation. In such a case, suicide becomes an "escape" from a prison of physical pain, emotional torment, and sexual abuse.

Lori was first raped by her father when she was ten; several times a week since that first May afternoon, he would sneak quietly down the hall, enter her room, latch her door, and lower his bulk into the double bed that was pushed underneath the window. Lori tried to think of anything else she could — the blossoms on the peach tree outside her window, the recipe for the cookies she had made in home ec, or the fabric she was going to choose for her new skirt — until, satisfied, her father went back along the darkened hallway. One night, not able to face any more of his abuse, she pretended to go to her room to bed; before he could make his traditional trip down the hall, she hung herself from her closet rod.

The Need for Sending Out A Distress Signal

In some cases — involving both attempted and completed suicides — the teenager doesn't really want to die. Instead, he is trying to say, "Notice me. I need help badly." Unfortunately, he feels isolated or estranged from those around him, and he is not

---

"What we see in the typical suicidal person is someone who has considered only one way out of his problems. We have to try to help him understand that there are many solutions besides suicide."

—*William Young, Executive Director, Sarasota Guidance Clinic*

able to communicate his need for help in a more appropriate way. His desperate act of self-destruction is the only way he knows. *(A special note: Pay attention to an adolescent who asks for help. Adolescence is normally a period of increasing independence and a desire for self-reliance. Asking for help is not a normal adolescent behavior. Most adolescents want privacy; most also want to make it on their own. You can consider an adolescent's plea for help as a serious sign of high suicidal risk.)*

The Desire to Manipulate Someone Else

In some cases, teenage suicide is an attempt to manipulate someone else. Such a person doesn't really want to die: she is using the suicide attempt as a way to get someone to behave differently (usually through guilt).

When Sherry's boyfriend told her he didn't want to see her anymore, she was frantic. She swallowed a few handfuls of assorted pills out of her mother's prescription bottles because she believed it would make him come back. She didn't intend on dying — but the drug interaction was fatal, and she wasn't discovered until morning, cold and lifeless in the corner of the bathroom where she had sunk to the floor.

The Desire to Punish Someone Else

In this case, the person really *does* want to die, because he sees it as the ultimate punishment for someone who has wronged him; if he lives, it would give the person a chance to redeem himself. Almost all cases of adolescent suicide that fall into this category involve an adolescent's desire to punish his or her

"More and more, violence is being accepted as a way of life in America. A lot of our youngsters are becoming numbed to violence without comprehending the irreversibility of death."

—*Dr. Pamela Cantor, President, American Association of Suicidology*

parents; very occasionally, the teenager wants to punish a teacher, coach, or friend.

Overwhelming Shame or Guilt

In many cases, the incident that prompts an adolescent's suicide may seem extremely minor to an adult; to the teenager involved, however, it is easier to face death than to face the risk of ridicule and rejection. It might be something as simple as being kicked off the debate team, scoring low on an important test, or stumbling and causing the relay team to lose the race.

Steve had consistently scored at the top of his ninth-grade science class; every time there was a test or an assignment, the teacher commented on his performance in front of the entire class. On a few occasions he had even read excerpts from Steve's paper or invited Steve to explain a complicated concept to the rest of the class. When they started the unit on animals, however, Steve had a difficult time remembering the long Latin names and comprehending the processes involved in cell division. When papers with drawings were required, Steve fell far below his usual score; the teacher invited Christine, usually a shy student, to share her paper with the class. When the unit test was given, Steve scored a full twenty points below his average. Wracked with a sense of failure and the belief that he would never again score well in science — his favorite subject — Steve tried to kill himself by taking a handful of the only prescription pills he could find in the house. Luckily, they weren't potent enough to kill him.

Poor Impulse Control

When confronted with an uncomfortable situation, a teenager may attempt or commit suicide on a whim. He may see the suicide only as an immediate way to solve a temporary problem. Because of poor impulse control, he follows through on his whim — and his decision is irreversible. Adolescents who have been successful in developing control over impulsive behavior are not as prone to suicide as those with poor impulse control.

Tunnel Vision

Judie Angell, a popular author who has written a number of books for and about teenagers, says that a leading cause of suicide among teenagers is tunnel vision. "Tunnel vision is the inability to see anything else in life but the loneliness and pain of that particular moment," she says. "It's the inability to step back and know that things will get better. Grown-ups know that you get over certain disappointments and setbacks, that they won't affect the rest of your life. But kids think, I wasn't invited to that party, or, I'm breaking up with my boyfriend, and they can't see beyond that." One teenager substantiates the tunnel vision theory when he admits, "It sounds crazy, but I think it's true — kids end up committing suicide to get out of taking their finals."

Exposure to Violence

Adolescents are being exposed to an ever-increasing range of violence in the movies, on television, and in music videos; gradually, many come to accept violence without thinking consciously about it. When they become angry at themselves or

"Teenagers watch television and see that life problems are presented and fixed in a half-hour program. It gives people an automatic sense that things should resolve quickly. But what happens in real life is that many problems don't resolve. You have to learn to live with them, to adapt and cope."

—*Dr. Mary Giffin, Medical Director, North Shore Mental Health Association, Northfield, Illinois*

hostile or they start hating themselves, it becomes easier for them to exercise violence against themselves. Too many children and teenagers are not being taught how to cope with violent impulses and how to avoid violent behavior.

Desire to Get Attention

A teenager who has tried unsuccessfully to get his parents' attention may, in one last desperate move, attempt suicide as a way of getting his parents to pay attention to him and his needs. Washington, D.C., psychiatrist Willie Hamlin says, "Parents are sometimes so busy working hard to provide the material things that they've neglected what the child really needs and wants — time, attention, love and affection. The child acts out with suicide attempts to get attention."

Striving for Perfection

A perfectionistic adolescent is setting himself up for failure — if he is anything less than perfect, he deems himself to be a miserable failure, a mediocre louse (even though he may in reality be an above-average achiever), and an unacceptable embarrassment. He becomes afraid to try anything new because he fears he will not be perfect at it; he hangs back instead of plunging into things that others find fun because he doesn't want to do a less-than-perfect job. He becomes lonely

"Many of these kids have poor coping mechanisms for the enormous stresses they face. When they become overwhelmed by pain, they can't imagine when things will be better in the future. They're too young to realize, 'This, too, shall pass.'"

—Dr. Michael Peck, Director, Youth Services and the Outpatient Clinic, Los Angeles Suicide Prevention Center

and isolated because he doesn't dare strike up a relationship — what if he blows it?

In the end, the adolescent who is striving for perfectionism achieves much less than he would have because of his fears and his failure to try. And the emotions associated with his desire to be "the best" can lead him to a shattering of self-esteem, causing feelings of worthlessness and inadequacy that may lead to suicide.

Unresolved Grief

The tremendous emotional baggage that accompanies grief can be too much for many teenagers to handle. Borrowing from a speaker at the 1985 National Conference on Youth Suicide, consider the following cases:

Twelve-year-old Cindy creased the scrap of notebook and shoved it across her desk toward Emily — but Cindy's fingering of the paper was too uncertain, and the note drifted to the floor. The home economics teacher paced methodically down the aisle between the wood and formica desks; a frown creased the corners of her mouth. All the girls in the class knew it was against the rule to pass notes, especially during an exam.

She picked up the creased scrap of notebook paper, unfolded it, and read in an uncertain hand, "I tried to kill myself last night. That's why I'm so dopey today."

She felt the chills run down her spine like a skittering bolt of lightning. She folded the scrap of paper back up and went back to the front of the room. She was too embarrassed to look Cindy in the eye. Instead, she turned the note over to the principal at the end of the class period; the principal, after studying the note for what seemed like an eternity, lifted the heavy phone receiver out of the cradle and dialed Cindy's house.

The next few weeks were a flurry of psychiatrists, doctors, and painful memories. Cindy's life started to unfold in alarming clarity. She remembered being beaten up by an older sister at the age of three. At seven, she tried to drown herself in the bathtub. ("Did you *really* want to die?" asked the astonished psychologist. "I wanted to end the pain," Cindy remembered, "but I desperately wanted to live.") At eleven, she was beaten and molested by her alcoholic father.

Cindy wasn't the only child in the family to be in crisis. She has a seven-year-old brother, but Chris wasn't bottling his grief up inside. He was letting it all out. Chris wasn't suicidal; he was homicidal. At the age of seven, he lunged out in attacks on his teachers, his classmates, even his parents; his aggression was intense and frightening.

The difference?

Cindy held her grief inside; Chris was letting his out.

Diane, an attractive nineteen-year-old college student, seemed to have a subconscious suicide wish: she would wake up in the middle of the night and discover that she had walked to the dresser, picked up a pair of scissors, and was gouging her flesh with the sharp blades.

Why?

When Diane was seven, she and two older sisters were left in charge of their two younger siblings, a two-year-old girl and a five-year-old boy. But she and her older sisters had more important things to do than be bothered by a couple of clinging preschoolers, so they went about the business of dolls and dressups. No one knew exactly how the fire started, or how long it had been blazing before the three girls discovered it. But when the smoke cleared and the last of the glowing embers was dampened by the coiling red fireman's hose, they found her. Two-year-old Jenny's scorched body lay twisted against the stairway.

The grief and guilt were overwhelming. Every year on the April anniversary of Jenny's death, their father lashed out in anger and recrimination to the three older sisters who had been lost in floppy-brimmed hats and lace handkerchiefs when the first traces of smoke curled up the stairs. Diane, crippled by unresolved grief, took to slashing herself in the still of the night. Her two older sisters expressed their grief in a different way: through an incestuous relationship with their abusive, punishing father.

Loss of Identity

Often hand-in-hand with unresolved grief is a loss of identity — but it can, and does, occur on its own. It is a wrenching, isolating kind of pain that can lead to suicide in an attempt to end the pain. More case studies from the 1985 National Conference on Youth Suicide illustrate.

Scott, a freshman in college, was discovered in his darkened dorm room one Friday night adjusting the noose of his bathrobe belt securely around his neck. He was distraught about getting caught, but agreed to the mandatory counseling the university health services prescribed.

It didn't take long to realize why Scott was suicidal. His father was a doctor. His mother was a lawyer. His brother was a dentist. His sister was a lawyer. Scott wanted to be a chef — but that was totally unacceptable to his family. Clear up until the moment they deposited his suitcases on the curb outside the dorm and drove away in a puff of exhaust fumes, his parents were scolding him about the indignity of being a chef. His father punctuated the shrill blasts of his mother with anecdotes about medical school and the importance of getting good grades right from the beginning. As he watched them pull away from the curb and merge into the traffic that disappeared around the corner, he shook his head. He didn't want to be a doctor. He wanted to be a chef.

Scott's counselor also discovered that Scott had a real talent for interior design — another profession that his parents had snorted over with disgust. One day, as Scott breezed through the door for his counseling session, he tossed his jacket on the back of a tattered chair and sighed, "This office is a mess!"

The minute he said it he was sorry. He braced himself emotionally, waiting for the outburst from his counselor.

Instead, the counselor leaned back in his chair, rubbed his chin, and said, "It is, isn't it? I've got some money from our department funds. It isn't much, but with some creativity it could go a long way. Will you help me fix this office up?"

For the first time, someone had given Scott the chance to accept himself as he was.

Jared had always been big for his age. In kindergarten, he towered above the other kids as they huddled around the teacher during story time. In the fifth grade, he was so tall that he was mistaken for a student at the nearby high school. And by the time he turned fifteen, the high school coach was thrusting a pair of cleated football shoes at Jared from across the counter in the boys' locker room.

Jared took the shoes with hesitation. He fingered the black laces, scraped a bit of dried mud from between the cleats. It was the last part of his uniform — his blue and gold jersey, his stained pants, the thick pads and tough plastic helmet. Jared dragged it all to a lonely spot on the bench and sat, alone. He didn't want to play football. The coach's rambling chalk strategies made no sense to Jared; he longed instead for the smooth coldness of a French horn pressed against his lips.

But Jared had no choice. His grandfather had been a pro football player. His father had been a coach at the local college. Even his mother had been on the football field, dancing frenetically on the sidelines in a cheerleading outfit. Jared's lot was cast — and his stomach rose in his throat as he imagined the damp, stinking bodies piled in a crushing heap on the grass outside.

Jared scooped the equipment up in his arms, bolted for the coach's counter, and threw the stuff of the gridiron back across the counter. The astonished coach started to protest, but Jared paced to the locker room door and slapped his hand against it sharply. With the muggy August air smothering him, he headed across the field. He wouldn't play the French horn — but he wouldn't play football, either. His mind raced to the hunting knife he had hidden between his mattresses at home, and he envisioned it slicing the flesh of both wrists . . . .

Dr. Ronald Maris of the University of South Carolina sums up the nature of youth suicide in the following way:

"Young suicides as a group are relatively unique in that they are more revenge motivated, anger, irritation,and impulsivity-based, have more negative interpersonal relations, make more nonfatal attempts, have more suicides and divorce in their families of origin, are less likely to have financial, work, or marital resources, involve more risk-taking, excessive drug and alcohol use, are more likely to be romantic and idealistic, have lower self-esteem, and fewer life accomplishments. This is all especially tragic, since most young suicides are among the least necessary premature deaths, generally with the greatest prospects for a pleasurable and productive future if their self-destructive crises can be weathered."

Myra Herbert, a social worker coordinator for Fairfax County, Virginia School District summarized her concern about the factors that may contribute to youth suicide in her testimony before the second session (Subcommittee on Juvenile Justice) on the Ninety-Eighth Congress.

"From my years of clinical practice with this age group and from the student groups held over the past year, there are numerous factors which emerge as important and should be given attention.

—Academics and academic pressure play a large part in young lives. The cost of college is overwhelming for many families and competition for scholarships is intense. Many students have jobs as well and know that colleges and universities place an importance on extra-curricular activities.

—Even the bright are pushed to the limit either by their own expectations or those of their families. Parental expectations, particularly unrealistic ones, play a large part in student stress.

—For those who are not bright or who clearly have learning difficulties, life appears bleak. In a world where those with college educations are not finding jobs, those who may just graduate from high school do not see great hope.

—Learning disability creates terrible frustration and students are often given unkind labels, such as dumb or stupid. We are not as a nation spending enough money researching the process of learning.

—A death of a parent or that of a close friend is a painful loss for an adolescent and can change the course of life.

—Being in a minority is often painful and lonely.

—An alcoholic parent is a damaging burden for an adolescent.

—Having a mentally or physically ill parent will often render a child troubled and depressed for much of his or her own life.

—The American emphasis on sports and sports achievement can leave many young people feeling inadequate because they cannot perform in this sphere.

—Divorce is not good for children. It is a searing, devastating experience for most children, and there is a necessity to handle it with much more care and concern than is often being exercised. Parents need more education.

—Living in combined families is not a story-book experience. It is fraught with peril and families need far more guidance than they are being given.

—Having two working parents proves to be a factor, particularly if a child is left alone a great deal or is left in charge of siblings. Not only is parental attention sometimes wanting, but studies on adults who have had this experience are beginning to show that it may leave an individual with unspecified fears, paranoid thinking, and a lack of social skills. Good care substitute plans deserve more consideration.

—Adjusting to a new society is sometimes mystifying to both children and their families, particularly when they are from a non-Western culture. Students get caught between parental behavioral dictates and the normal adolescent desire to emulate peers.

—Mobility and the transiency of our national population is often creating failure and misery for our yong people. In Fairfax County, we have a large governmental population, foreign service and State Department families, military families, and large corporation executives who seem to move every two or three years. In addition, one of the perils of affluence is the need to move to a larger, nicer house. Divorce also often means a location change. Some of our schools empty and refill by as much as 50 percent every year. Admittedly that is not typical of the national picture, but it is not atypical either of many urban areas. Children report moving as much as nine times in fourteen years. There are two dangers in this; one is that students are constantly changing school programs and, particularly if academics do not come easily, they give up somewhere along the way. The second is that they lose their friends and this is particularly difficult after the age of twelve. Coming into a new school can be a nightmare for many, and families often report severe behavioral changes.

When one begins to realize that many of our teenagers are experiencing several of these factors at the same time, the strains upon them become evident. We must as a society look at what we are doing to our children."

Warning Signs and Symptoms of Suicidal Adolescents

Suicide often comes as a great shock to the survivors — they may have had some inkling that the adolescent was unhappy or going through a "rough" period, but *they didn't expect the teenager to kill himself.*

Most often, they *should* have expected it. Experts believe that approximately 90 percent of those who commit suicide give clues about it first. Unfortunately, people don't recognize the clues. They fail to respond.

Experts have identified several "precipitating factors" that seem to commonly precede suicide. According to Dr. David Shaffer, professor of psychiatry and pediatrics at the New York State Psychiatric Institute of the Columbia College of Physicians and Surgeons, the following often precede suicide by a teenager.

—**Disciplinary crisis.** More than one-third of all teenage suicides, says Dr. Shaffer, are in response to a disciplinary crisis. But these teenagers don't kill themselves *following* an intense or demeaning episode of discipline. Instead, they kill themselves *in anticipation* of the discipline. Most, he says, kill themselves in the moment between realizing they are in trouble and wondering exactly what the consequences will be.

—Losing face with peers. A little more than one-fifth of teenage suicides may follow an episode in which the adolescent loses face with his or her peers. A star quarterback may fumble the ball, giving the opposition the winning touchdown of the state championship game. A girl may be the only one in her group not invited to the junior prom. A fifteen-year-old bragging about his prowess and his ability to outsmart his parents may be picked up by the police and placed in detention for driving his father's car. A girl anxious for admission to an Ivy League school finds that she is the only one in her circle of friends who did not make the minimum score on the Scholastic Achievement Test.

—Argument with a parent. While it is much less common — involving only about 13 percent of teenage suicides — argument with a parent may serve as a precipitating factor to adolescent suicide. Even in those cases, it may not be the argument itself that precipitates the suicide but the complex relationship that has led to the argument (including feelings of loneliness, isolation from the family unit, and so on).

—Imitation. While imitation is least common of the major precipitating factors, it can and does lead to teenage suicide in about 10 percent of the cases. The adolescent may read about suicide, see a suicide in movies or on television (as in the frequently cited examples of *An Officer and a Gentleman*), or be acquainted with another teenager who commits suicide.

The incidence of suicide as imitation increases if the suicide victim was well-known, charistmatic, or well-liked and if the suicide itself was heroic or well publicized.

The most commons set of precipitants, says Shaffer, includes a long history of failures; a history of aggression; a history of substance abuse (approximately 50 percent are impaired by drug or alcohol abuse at the time of the suicide); a personality, most common among boys, that is rigid, perfectionistic, and marked by performance anxiety (a teenage boy may take an important test and then kill himself *before* he finds out the results); and a history, most common among girls, of eating disorders.

Just as every suicide is intensely personal and unique, every suicide has its own set of individual clues. Sometimes a single clue will be given; in other cases, a person may give a host of clues before finally committing suicide. The following may occur alone or in combination with other clues in a teenager who is seriously contemplating suicide:

—The adolescent may become unconcerned about his personal welfare. He may fail to take necessary precautions; a fifteen-year-old boy who always fastened his seat belt may stop doing so. He may not make moves to improve his own comfort. He may not defend his position in a dispute at school — when he is called in by the principal for questioning about possible involvement in a drug ring, he shrugs his shoulders and fails to offer his perfectly legitimate alibi. He seems to be saying, "I don't matter; who cares about me, anyway?"

—He may show one or more signs of serious depression. Watch for the following:

—Sadness
—Fluctuations between indifference and apathy on the one hand, and talkativeness and interest on the other
—Anger and rage, usually expressed by a verbal attack and sarcasm instead of through physical attack

---

"In a society where a young person attempts suicide every 90 seconds and another succeeds every 90 minutes, you may save a lot of lives if you learn to recognize the warning signs."

—*Emergency Medicine*

—Sensitivity, especially characterized by the tendency to overreact to criticism

—A feeling that he cannot live up to his ideals

—Poor self-esteem

—Feelings of helplessness and decreased peer support; friends who were once important are no longer relied on

—Intense ambivalence between wanting dependence and independence; on the one hand, the teenager yearns to be independent and strong, while on the other hand she frequently seeks the protection offered by her parents and teachers

—Feelings of emptiness or meaninglessness in life

—Restlessness and agitation

—Pessimism about the future

—Death wishes, suicide ideas, suicide plans, or suicide attempts

—Rebellious refusal to work in class or to cooperate in general, both inside and outside the home

—Sleep disturbances

—Increased or decreased appetite

—Weight gain or loss

—Disturbing physical symptoms (such as a persistent headache) that cannot be explained by physical causes

—The inability to play or have fun

—Complaints about always being tired or bored, accompanied by a lack of interest or concentration

—**Many adolescents give verbal clues.** Sometimes, they actually and directly threaten suicide ("I think I'll just kill

The teenager who has reached the point of seriously considering suicide never fails to send out warning signals."

—*Dr. Mary Giffin, Medical Director, North Shore Mental Health Association, Northfield, Illinois*

myself!"). Often, though, the clues are more subtle and difficult to pinpoint. "You'll be sorry that you didn't let me go to the prom when I'm not around anymore!" "You'd all be better off if I were dead." "Soon I won't have to worry about my math grades anymore." "Don't worry, you won't have to be paying for my music lessons much longer." "I don't think I need to talk to the counselor at school; things won't be like this for very much longer."

Clues like that are easy to miss. A troubled student who tells you that he won't have to worry about his math grades anymore could be saying that he plans to commit suicide, or he may be saying that in six weeks the semester will be over and he will be out of the class. You need to judge what is said in the context of how the teenager is behaving and what other kinds of clues he may be giving.

—**A teenager who has not had much trouble may suddenly become accident-prone. Why?** *They only seem like accidents.* A series of bothersome accidents may actually be half-hearted suicide attempts that failed, or they may be minor attempts at self-destruction that the person is "practicing" with in order to build up courage for the real thing. The accidents may also be unconscious attempts at self-destruction.

Cindy's parents were surprised when they started reconstructing the events that had preceded her suicide by slashing her wrists: when they stopped to think about it now, they remembered a number of occasions when Cindy had cut herself. Once, when four or five of the neighborhood kids had

---

"I do not believe that young people will be incited to suicidal behavior by hearing about it, but I do firmly believe that they will continue to be prevented from helping themselves and others by being falsely 'protected' from the subject."

—*Francine Klagsbrun, author of* Too Young To Die: Youth and Suicide

been playing outside, she had come in with a deep cut on her forearm; she told them she had fallen against the jagged edge of a broken bottle, but she seemed unusually unconcerned about the cut, which was bleeding heavily. A week or so later, she was chopping vegetables for dinner when she "accidentally" sliced into the skin across three of her knuckles. Still later, she carved an ugly gash behind her knee — allegedly when she became distracted while shaving her legs.

—**The teenager may undergo a sudden change in his habits, attitudes, or personality.** A fifteen-year-old who was once confident and aggressive may become passive and withdrawn. A high school senior who was always talkative and happy may become sullen and quiet. A sixteen-year-old girl who had always been meticulous about keeping her room clean (sometimes to the point of fanaticism) suddenly neglects it completely: her mother is surprised to see clothes strewn on the floor and draped over the chair, remnants of half-eaten snacks congealed against greasy paper plates, and the wastebasket overflowing with wads of paper, empty pantyhose packages, and shreds of completed homework assignments.

—**The adolescent may suffer a sudden or pronounced decline in school.** Everyone suffers through a rough period once in awhile, especially when starting to study a new subject or starting in a new school. But you should watch for the teenager who hasn't changed school subjects, hasn't changed teachers, and hasn't switched to a new school but is suddenly having an extremely difficult time keeping up. Look for duration, too — a thirteen-year-old who has always been good at math may have particular problems understanding a certain calculation in his algebra class, but the next week he will be "back to normal." If a problem exists, however, the thirteen-year-old math whiz will suddenly begin to fail his algebra class without reasonable cause, and he will not bounce back within a few weeks.

—**Be alert for signs of confusion, such as difficulty in concentrating or difficulty in thinking clearly.** The person may either be deeply depressed or may be so preoccupied with thoughts of his suicide that he can't concentrate on anything else. Watch for a teenager who seems withdrawn and "in another world" when he's with his family or a group of his friends.

—Many suicidal teenagers begin to neglect their appearance and hygiene; after usually being well-groomed and well-dressed, they may suddenly become dirty, disheveled, or poorly groomed.

Jennifer had been the family "clothes horse" since she turned thirteen; she wouldn't disgrace her closet with anything that didn't bear a designer label. She eagerly babysat for the neighbors and did odd jobs around the house that could increase her allowance; with greedy enthusiasm, she fingered the dollar bills in her hiding place until she had enough to buy the sweater she had been admiring at the mall or the cropped jeans like Lisa wore. She consistently got up an hour before the rest of the family, and spent it in the bathroom, with pots and potions and tins of vibrant colors spread on the tile counter before her. The money that she didn't spend on clothes and makeup was spent on frequent haircuts and an occasional highlighting.

Two months before her suicide from a drug overdose, Jennifer changed markedly. She slept late, often until minutes before the school bus rumbled up to the corner; sometimes she didn't even wash her face, and her mother noticed that she would leave for school with black mascara smudged beneath her eyes. She rarely did more than drag a comb through her hair. Her mother also noticed that she often wore the same

---

"In the face of these danger signals, it is extremely important to remember that there is no suicide 'type.' Preconceived notions about who might or might not commit suicide must be pushed to the side."

—*A. Russell Lee, Director of Family Therapy Training, Pacific Medical Center, and Charlotte P. Ross, President/Executive Director, Youth Suicide National Center*

clothes for three or four days in a row — unheard of for Jennifer — until they were stained or wrinkled beyond belief. She even stopped wearing socks. Her mother thought she was going through a "phase," until she found Jennifer curled up in the corner of her closet, dead from a bottle of prescription painkillers.

— **Watch out for signs that the teenager is "putting his affairs in order."** He may suddenly start to organize an interest in finishing up some long-standing projects — such as a model airplane or an intricately smocked dress. Especially serious is the teenager who starts parting with treasured possessions. A sixteen-year-old girl who thrusts her favorite sweater at her younger sister (after guarding the sweater jealously for a year and threatening anyone who touched it) with the words, "Here, you take this. I won't be needing it anymore" is probably at extremely high risk for suicide.

— **The teenager may lose interest in friends or activities that used to interest him.** An avid soccer fan may no longer want to participate in soccer; a girl who once loved playing the flute drops out of orchestra class. You may notice that the teenager is becoming increasingly withdrawn socially; he may refuse to socialize with friends he once enjoyed. He may look for excuses to avoid other people, especially in organized activities.

Linda had always loved going to the show on Friday nights; she looked forward to it all week, and on Thursday afternoon she and three of her friends pored over the movie selection of the newspaper, making their careful decision. She laid her clothes out on her bed before she went to school on Friday morning so that she could sail home, bound up the stairs, and be ready to go with plenty of time to spare. She always counted a few quarters out of her bank so she could buy popcorn, and her bedroom walls were papered with movie posters.

About a month before her suicide, Linda lost interest in going to the movies on Friday nights. When her friends tried to persuade her to go, she would always come up with a weak excuse — she had to study for a test the next Monday, her Mom needed her to clean the bathrooms, she had a headache and wanted to rest. When her father surprised her with the latest movie poster, she propped it in a dusty corner near her bed instead of tacking it up immediately with the usual ceremonial flair. Her parents assumed she had had some kind of an argument with the three girls who always went with her to the movies.

— **The person may joke about suicide.** Suicide, of course, is no laughing matter — but he may be trying to clothe it in humor while he "tries it on" and assesses other people's reactions to it.

— **Many suicide victims become physically ill, are diagnosed as having serious or terminal illnesses, or suffer from the physical symptoms of depression.** Be especially watchful of a teenager who seems to have a number of illnesses (even minor ones) that affect many different body systems; a danger sign may be given by a teenager who suddenly develops persistent headaches, pain in the joints, a gnawing stomach ache, a nagging cough, and chronic fatigue. Watch, too, for an adolescent who seems to be taking an inordinate amount of time to recover from an illness or accident: Amy, a deeply depressed fifteen-year-old who was having suicidal thoughts and who had even planned to kill herself, astounded her doctor and her parents by languishing with a strep throat for almost two months.

— **The teenager may suddenly start having difficulty in communicating with other people.** He may have a difficult time expressing his thoughts and feelings; he may not have an interest in listening to others; he may have a difficult time

"Recognizing suicidal behaviors — and taking them seriously — may be all that's needed to prevent a suicide attempt."

—*Sharon Valente, RN, Department of Nursing, UCLA*

concentrating. Suicidal people may especially have a hard time establishing eye contact with others. Speech may be slow, faltering, or stumbling.

Adolescence is often a time of strained communications; many teenagers have a difficult time talking freely and openly with parents, teachers, or friends. It is important to allow for this "normalcy." What you are watching for is a *change* or a sudden shift in the teenager's style of communicating: beware of the teenager who was once talkative and eager to share ideas and who has become sullen, quiet, and withdrawn, unwilling to talk to his parents or to speak up in class.

— The person may seem to develop an unusually intense interest in what is happening to others or how others are feeling.

Not long before his unsuccessful suicide attempt, Cory seemed to become obsessed with his problems at school. Nothing was able to distract him, even momentarily — not even the news that a favorite grandmother was dying of congestive heart failure. While the rest of the family members gathered at her bedside, spent time talking to her on the phone, and spent hours talking about their memories of her, Cory talked only about a teacher "who hated him" and his inability to become part of a popular peer group.

"It's a myth that suicide happens out of the blue, or that it's an impulsive act. It may appear impulsive at the time, but if you talk to these teens — the ones who luckily survive — you can see that there was a buildup over time. They'd tried to resolve what they've felt in various ways, but each teenager progressively felt that there was no one who understood."

—Linda Share, Crossroads Hospital, Van Nuys, California

— **Certain physical complaints are common in suicidal people.** Watch for signs of sleep disturbances, anorexia (a marked loss of appetite, with or without nausea), profound and rapid weight loss, fatigue, loss of energy, muscle weakness, constipation, headache, dizziness, numbness of the extremities, blurred vision, and a burning of the eyes. Again, you are watching for a change — don't jump to the conclusion that a teenager who complains of headaches is suicidal if he has been bothered by headaches for a number of years. Suicidal people have often convinced themselves that their discomfort is a permanent condition, and that they will not recover from whatever is ailing them.

— **A suicidal teenager may weep easily, with seemingly little provocation.** Usually such overemotional response is a sign of depression, but it can also be a sign of deep anguish or upset.

— **The teenager may become preoccupied with something that happened in the past, usually some past wrongdoing or "sin" that he committed.** He may express how "bad" he is because of what happened (even though, to you, he has obviously overcome the problem and gone on to live a happy and productive life). Usually, the wrongdoing or "sin" seems insignificant to you, but seems overwhelming in its severity to the suicidal person.

"Most young people give clues to their suicidal thoughts. These clues may include marked changes in behavior — they may become secretive, or they may give away cherished possessions. The clues may be verbal — an accusing, 'You don't care if I'm alive or dead.' If such remarks do not evoke a sympathetic response to their feelings, youngsters may go on to threaten suicide directly. Such threats should always be taken seriously."

—*Youth Suicide National Center*

Sixteen-year-old Rob suddenly became obsessed with the time three years earlier that he and two friends had smuggled a few Valium out of his parent's medicine cabinet and had swilled them down with water to see how it felt. Nothing had stemmed from the incident, and Rob had not gone on to abuse drugs — but he couldn't seem to forgive himself for the incident. He became disgusted at himself, and before long the Valium itself wasn't the only issue — he became tormented that he had been dishonest, that he had violated his parents' trust, that he had picked the lock on the medicine cabinet, that he had stolen from his parents. No one — including his parents — could understand his upset at remembering the petty theft; in fact, his parents found it almost amusing that he could be so tormented by such a minor problem. Their amusement ended when he shot himself in the same bathroom where he had pilfered the precious Valium.

While some teenagers become obsessed with minor infractions, others begin to concentrate on past problems that were real and disturbing. During the summer between her ninth- and tenth-grade years in school, Kim became pregnant. After hours of counseling with her parents, her doctor, and counselors at school, Kim decided to give the baby up for adoption. Her pregnancy progressed without incident until the last few months, when she turned to drugs and alcohol because of mounting confusion, pressure, and demands. Her doctor had worked with an attorney to find adoptive parents; a couple in their thirties who had tried for seven years to have a baby were chosen, and they eagerly awaited the birth as they splashed the nursery with paint and stained a wooden Jenny Lind crib.

The tiny dark-haired girl was born seven weeks early with multiple problems and defects; some of them, her doctor hinted, may have been because of the drugs and alcohol that Kim had ingested during her last trimester and during the early days of her pregnancy before she learned of her condition. Kim stayed in the hospital for four days, and anxiously asked the nurses to wheel her by the glass incubator almost hourly. Her tiny baby lay in a maze of tubes and needles, the heart monitor beeping out a steady rhythm while the respirator whirred the haunting breaths. A few days after Kim was discharged from the hospital, her baby died. The adoptive parents were overwhelmed with grief, and Kim herself was distraught.

Now, two years later, she seemed obsessed with her "bad" behavior — because she was "bad," she had "killed" her baby. She had been solely responsible for the disappointment and grief of the young couple who had waited eagerly for the birth. She — a "bad person who had done bad things" — needed to pay for her sins. So while her father made intricate revisions on an architectural sketch one June afternoon, Kim leapt from the fourteenth-floor window of his office building: two years to the day after her baby died.

— **The teenager may become preoccupied with a poor self-image; she may dwell on her faults, failures, betrayals, errors, or poor judgment, ignoring or not acknowledging any positive traits.** He may seem convinced that he is worthless or that he is a "burden" to someone else.

Paul suddenly seemed to become preoccupied with the fact that he was not able to make the cut for the school band. During junior high school, he had dabbled with the trombone, never taking it too seriously; while other students his age stayed inside practicing, Paul had tossed a worn football or carefully pruned the dwarf peach trees that lined the back fence. Now, Paul was convinced that he was worthless because he couldn't play the trombone well enough to be accepted into the marching band — even though he was a gifted math student, a promising football player, and a natural at horticulture. He simply couldn't see any positives in his life: it was all overshadowed by his one negative.

— **A suicidal teenager may seem to be "sowing his wild oats" or "making hay while the sun shines."** He may go on a shopping spree, spending all the money he had been saving for a trip to the Super Bowl game. He may suddenly get involved in dozens of activities that previously didn't interest him — almost as though he needs to squeeze as much frenetic activity into the little time he has left.

—An adolescent who becomes suicidal may do so in response to intense stress or a life crisis. Look for signs of unusually difficult problems that have occurred recently, such as the loss of a parent (through death, separation, or divorce), the death of a close friend, serious illness or injury, loss of religious convictions, and threat of trouble with the law, or any other problem that could cause stress. Especially look for a teenager who has recently suffered the loss of a friend or family member to suicide.

— A suicidal teenager may become preoccupied with thoughts of death. She may talk excessively about death or read books about death. She may talk about her funeral and what she would like to have included as part of her funeral. She may frequently talk about what it would be like to die or what life after death will be like. Such a teenager is usually still torn between life and death, and is trying to make the decision which way to go.

— A suicidal teenager may suddenly begin using drugs or alcohol excessively. While many teenagers experiment or use these substances on an occasional basis, a suicidal teenager may become entrenched in a pattern of abuse.

— While the majority of teenagers who commit suicide are not victims of mental illness, some do suffer from problems such as schizophrenia or paranoia. Most experts estimate that mental illness is involved in only about 10 percent of adolescent suicides. A teenager who demonstrates signs of serious mental illness — such as hallucinations, delusions, or talking to herself — probably needs help.

— Teenagers who previously had an acceptable or desirable relationship with their parents may suddenly develop interpersonal problems with their parents if they begin to go through a suicidal crisis.
Kathy's father had died when she was eight, and since that time she had enjoyed a close and loving relationship with her mother. The two of them had been able to talk about almost

anything, and Kathy respected her as a confidant, counselor, and friend. One of the signs of Kathy's impending suicide was the total obliteration of that relationship: suddenly, she viewed her mother with hostility, resentment, and suspicion. When her mother tried to talk to her about her friends or what was happening at school, Kathy was convinced that she was "prying" or "snooping" instead of continuing the kind of relationship they had both once enjoyed.

— **A suicidal adolescent may display sudden and marked changes in eating and sleeping habits.**
Jim had always loved to stay up late, begging his parents to let him linger just a little longer — until the news was over, then until he had heard the editorial comment. Even after retiring to his room the light would filter out into the hall from under his door, and they could hear him quietly working on a few private projects. Obviously, it was tough to get him up and going in the morning, but the next night the scenario was always repeated.

A few weeks before his suicide, Jim started voluntarily going to bed early in the evening. On several occasions, he didn't even wait around for dinner; instead, he would drag up the stairs, shut his door against the world, and bury himself in the hand-stitched quilts. It was still difficult to get him up in the morning. His father commented that Jim couldn't seem to get enough sleep.

— **A teenager who is close to committing suicide may suddenly become violent or rebellious after a history of being compliant and passive.** A common problem is running away or repeated truancy at school.

— **Be particularly suspicious or watchful of a teenager who suddenly cheers up and becomes a whirlwind of animated, enthusiastic activity after a period of oppressing gloom.** What does it mean? It can often mean that a deeply troubled and seriously depressed adolescent has finally decided to take the final, fatal step of suicide — and that decision in itself is a relief. The ensuing cheerfulness and seeming enthusiasm may be a reflection of the lifting of that burden: the decision has been made, the act will be completed soon, and the teenager doesn't have to worry about it anymore.

— **A suicidal teenager may exhibit sudden promiscuity, sudden weight loss, sudden and persistent irritability, and a sudden isolation accompanied by morose behavior and withdrawal.**

Obviously, most of these signs can be present in the life of a teenager who is *not* contemplating suicide; they do not always indicate suicide, nor do all adolescents who commit suicide give these specific indicators. When you notice a combination of these signs or when you observe sudden and marked changes, you should take special note. And remember — it doesn't hurt to ask. You might say, "I've noticed that you've really seemed to lose your appetite lately. Is something bothering you?"

Warning Signs in Teenage Suicides
Can Be Detected:
A Word from the American Academy of Pediatrics

Adolescent suicide has become a national concern, capturing the attention of television fiction as well as hard news reports. The media recently have reported the startling news that teen suicides sometimes occur in clusters — one suicide in a community often can stimulate a string of suicides among young people attending the same high school or group of schools.

Suicidal tendencies are detectable. Studies show that teenagers who consider killing themselves give warning signs before their suicide attempts. The warning signs include many standard indications of depression:

—Noticeable change in eating and sleeping habits
—Withdrawal from friends and family
—Persistent boredom
—Decline in quality of school work
—Violent or rebellious behavior
—Running away
—Drug and alcohol abuse
—Unusual neglect of personal appearance
—Difficulty concentrating
—Radical personality change
—Psychosomatic complaints

A teenager who is planning to commit suicide might give verbal hints such as "I won't be a problem for you much longer," "Nothing matters," or "It's no use." The adolescent also might make "final arrangements" such as giving away favorite possessions or throwing away personal mementos.

Teenagers who commit suicide often feel that nobody needs them — that nobody cares. Many adolescent suicides occur shortly after a loss of some kind — the death of a friend, the breakup with a boyfriend or girlfriend, or parents' divorce.

Some estimates hold that adolescent suicide is the third leading cause of death among teenagers. Parents, brothers or sisters, friends, and teachers who notice any signs that indicate the possibility of suicide should discuss them with the child or teenager. Don't be afraid that talking about suicide will cause the youngster to do it. Frank discussions about his or her feelings can have the opposite effect. Professional help should be sought if there is reason for serious concern. Sources of help include pediatricians, child psychiatrists, "hot line" services, local medical societies, and other physicians. Many medical organizations recommend that parents join children in viewing television broadcasts about suicide to discuss their feelings afterward. Most important, if your child ever talks about committing suicide, don't dismiss the youngster's comments. Deal with his or her concerns in an open manner. Take action promptly.

—*Reprinted from* Young Health, *American Academy of Pediatrics, Winter 1985.*

Assessing Suicidal Risk

Once you've determined that an adolescent may be suicidal, there are some important things you need to do. You need to *ask* him, directly and in a straightforward way, if he is considering killing himself or if he has thought about suicide. That may seem extremely difficult to do, but it is critical: the teenager is probably ambivalent about death, and you may be able to nudge him toward life if you can get it out in the open.

Some people worry about discussing suicide; they are afraid that they will plant the idea in someone who wasn't considering suicide to begin with. That's not likely. The suicidal thoughts are probably already there — and if they're not, your simple question won't plant them there.

What if the person admits that he is considering suicide? What then?

Your job is to determine how serious he is. One point needs to be made: you should take *every* suicide threat seriously. Many people who commit suicide talk about it first. You should *never* ignore or dismiss a suicide threat. As you may guess, however, there are people who are much more intent or capable of killing themselves than others. You can pinpoint those who are at extremely high risk by asking a few questions and considering a few factors:

Do you have a plan for committing suicide? A teenager might have vague, fleeting thoughts about suicide, but no concrete plan; if so, his risk is low. If he has more frequent thoughts and has had occasional ideas about a specific plan, his risk is greater. At high risk is the teenager who thinks a great deal about suicide and has formulated a detailed, carefully thought-out plan. ("I am going to take Dad's handgun out of his bottom dresser drawer, borrow the car, drive down to the marshes near the lake, lock the doors, and shoot myself through the mouth. I'm going to do it on a Friday night when everyone is out late, so they won't miss me until the next morning.")

The person is obviously at a much higher risk if the method he has chosen is a reliably lethal one — such as a gun — and if he has access to the equipment he needs to carry out his plan.

Have you ever tried to commit suicide before? If the answer is yes, the teenager is at an extremely high risk — even if previous attempts seemed half-hearted. An adolescent who chooses a nonlethal method the first time and fails will probably be more careful to "do it right" the next time.

Do you plan on trying to commit suicide again? Will you use the same method the next time, or have you chosen a new one? If the teenager has chosen a new method and admits to planning to use it, find out as much as you can. If, for example, she tried to slash her wrists before but is now planning on shooting herself, find out everything you can. If she has a gun and

---

"Suicidal thoughts, as studies have shown, aren't unusual. Almost everyone, at some point, has had at least a brief thought about suicide. As one teen recently said, 'Sure, I've had the fleeting thought that if I were dead, I wouldn't have to deal with this any more. But that's all it was, or ever could be — a fleeting thought.' "

—Aurora Mackey

ammunition, knows how to use it, and can supply the details about a specific plan, she is at high risk.

How do you feel about the fact that you failed to complete your suicide before? What made it a failure? Find out how he was rescued — and whether he *intended* to be rescued. A person who wanted to be rescued and felt relieved about it is at a lower risk than a person who is hostile and angry about being rescued and who was accidentally discovered and saved. A high risk would be suffered by a seventeen-year-old who took a bottle of sleeping pills while his parents were on a trip in another state: they had left him in charge of his younger sister, and he had sent her twenty miles away to a friend's house for the night, but he had been accidentally discovered by unexpected visitors. He didn't intend on being alive; he is alive by accident instead. You can bet he'll be more careful this time.

How do you feel about your parents (or other significant people in your life)? Those at low risk will report a healthy, vigorous relationship with their parents, close relatives, favorite teachers, or friends. At high risk are those who say they feel isolated, cut off, withdrawn, or unimportant to their parents or other significant people. They may tell you that they are a burden, that their parents would be better off without them, or that their parents don't care about them.

Has something recently happened that really troubled you? Low-risk teenagers might indicate some low levels of stress but

---

"In evaluating danger, be aware that as a general rule, the more specific the plan, the greater and more imminent the danger. If detailed plans have been made and the means of suicide obtained, the danger is not only great — it is immediate."

—Charlotte P. Ross and A. Russell Lee, M.D.

won't be able to relate specific, catastrophic events that have caused them extreme distress. High-risk teenagers, on the other hand, have probably suffered recent stressful experiences, such as failing in school, losing a part-time job, having a parent die, breaking up with a girlfriend, or watching parents go through a divorce.

Do you drink alcohol or use drugs? If so, high risk exists.

Are you physically ill? Have you been to see a doctor within the last few months? Teenagers at high risk are those who are suffering from a chronic illness, those who are suffering from a particularly painful illness, and those who have a variety of less serious illnesses that affect a number of different body systems. At even greater risk is the teenager who *thinks* he is ill and who goes to doctors frequently in an attempt to get some kind of a diagnosis.

Do you often feel hostile? Hostility generally signals a high risk. And the degree of hostility can usually be directly correlated to the success of a suicide attempt: a person who is filled with extreme hostility will usually choose a dramatic, shocking way of committing suicide, one that will have the greatest impact on the surv'vors.

How long have you been thinking about suicide? If a teenager tells you that her suicidal thoughts have been fleeting and infrequent over a period of just a few weeks, she is at a

---

"No one knows what or where the line is that separates the thought from the action itself. If we knew why one teenager thinks about it, and another teenager acts on the thought, we'd all be in a better position to spot the kid who's about to go over the edge."

—*Arnold Rothstein, Los Angeles, Clinical Social Worker*

lower risk than a teenager who says that he has seriously thought about suicide for two months. In an adult, you can consider a person who has thought of suicide for only a few weeks as a low risk. Unfortunately, teenagers are different. Teenagers tend to be more impulsive, plus there's another factor: teenagers tend to have what one expert has called "tunnel vision." They tend to think that their problems, however minor, will never go away — they don't have the ability to see down the road six months, when everyone will have forgotten that someone didn't make the football team.

Do you know anyone who has committed suicide? If so, consider the teenager to be at high risk. Especially high risk is indicated by teenagers who have lost an immediate family member to suicide and teenagers whose town has experienced several recent adolescent suicides (the "cluster suicide" effect).

Have you ever tried to get help before, and would you consider getting help now? You can consider the teenager to be at a low risk if she sought out help before, had a successful experience, and is eager and willing to be helped now. At high risk is the teenager who sought out help before but had a discouraging or unsuccessful experience with therapists or therapy programs. At extremely high risk is the adolescent who

---

"A very deadly act always reflects an ambivalence. A person who makes a suicide attempt is usually very determined to die, but once they feel the poison in their body or have that moment of realization about what they've done, the other side of their ambivalence becomes a very real part of that experience, and they don't want to do it. Some people see that and say, 'Oh, they weren't really serious.' . . . You can't really say that — because they are serious. About both feelings."

—Dr. Kim Smith, Codirector, The Menninger Suicide Research Project

firmly believes that she is beyond help — that no one wants to help, that nothing anyone can do will help, or that no help is available.

Is there someone in your life who provides you with support? If a teenager can name one or more people who provide strong support, he is at lower risk than if he can think of no one who functions in a supportive role. He is at high risk if he believes that no one stands between him and total abandonment and emotional desolation. Also at high risk is the teenager who tells you that an important support has been removed — whether through death, separation, abandonment, or changes in the style of the relationship.

What do you expect death to be like? Lower on the risk scale is the teenager who has a pretty accurate perception of death — who knows that death can be painful or frightening and who understands clearly that death is final and irreversible. At high risk is the teenager who tells you that death will be peaceful, nurturing, or will bring about some kind of relief; many suicidal adolescents don't really comprehend that they will *die*, but instead think they will enter into some kind of a romanticized state. According to Dr. Herbert Brown, instructor of psychiatry at the Cambridge Hospital, Harvard Medical School, these are at the highest risk of completing their suicidal intentions.

When you look ahead to the future, what do you see? If an adolescent talks about the future with some hope and optimism, he is probably a low risk. At high risk is the teenager who expresses dark depression, a sense of hopelessness, a feeling of powerlessness in directing his own life, or a pervading sense of worthlessness. Curt, a low risk, may talk in general terms about his going to college, completing law school, and practicing corporate law; Elaine, a high risk, may tell you that she can't imagine the future and that nothing is going to work out for her.

Have you been feeling depressed? For how long? Experts agree that depression is a major factor leading to suicide among all ages, and especially among adolescents. A high-risk adolescent will describe several symptoms of depression to you, which may include loss of appetite, despondency, sadness, weight loss, decreased sexual activity, confusion, chronic fatigue, sleep disorders, and various vague physical complaints.

Depression is a pretty accurate determinant of suicide, but the length of depression can be deceptive. Generally, high risk is indicated by a teenager who has been deeply depressed for a long period of time — in other words, someone who isn't suffering from a "normal" case of the blues that lasts for a few days or even a few weeks. But at even higher risk is a teenager who tells you that he has been deeply depressed for some time but feels like he is pulling out of it. As discussed, he might have finally made the decision to end his life, and he might finally be getting back some of the energy he needs to carry through with his plan. In essence, you should consider any seriously depressed teenager to be at considerable risk.

Do you really want to die? You'll find the answer to this question to be astounding. You can face a teenager who has the most brutal plan for ending his own life, and he may look you straight in the eye and tell you he doesn't really want to die. He is probably looking for a way to end his pain or an answer to his problems — and he figures he will have to die in the bargain. You'll discover what the researchers call **"ambivalence"**: he wants to live, but he wants to die. How far he swings to one extreme or the other can be a clue to risk. If he is basically positive about his world and admits a wish to survive, he is less of a risk than the teenager who is gloomy and negative and expresses the wish to die. Several studies quoted at the 1985 National Conference on Youth Suicide suggested that a teenager who expresses the desire to die will make more serious suicide attempts and will make them more frequently.

Can you use risk factors to predict suicide?

Some researchers think so — and one speaker at the 1985 National Conference on Youth Suicide, Dr. Jerome H. Motto, professor of psychiatry at the University of California at San Francisco School of Medicine, gave a simple, seven-point checklist that parents, teachers, and friends can use to "predict" suicidal behavior:

Current suicidal plan (specific, well-planned-out suicide plan that includes the date, time, circumstances, and method)

Prior suicidal behavior

Resources (does he have the resources necessary to carry out his plan — a gun? Knife? Knowledge to connect a hose from his car's exhaust pipe, and the hose with which to do it?)

Gender (men commit suicide three times more often than women)

Stress (stress is not a good predictor because what stresses you may not stress me)

Symptoms (don't use psychiatric illness symptoms as a predictor: only 12 percent of all suicides manifest any symptoms at all)

Age (adolescents between fifteen and twenty-four are at considerable risk, as are the elderly)

Dr. Motto concluded that depression — long accepted as a

"The first step toward prevention is to bring suicide out into the open. Troubled kids often don't have the ability to look ahead and may regard death as a solution to their problems. By discussing their fears, they learn they have options they never imagined."

—*Thomas Barrett, School Psychologist and Initiator of The Cherry Creek Suicide Prevention Project, Denver*

behavior that is consistent with suicidal behavior — is *descriptive*, not *predictive*. In other words, you can see that a suicidal person is depressed, but you cannot say that all depressed people are suicidal. Depression may describe many suicidal people, but it does not help predict which of those people will ultimately commit suicide.

Suicide Methods Most Often Used By Teenagers

The choice of methods among adolescents tends to vary, depending on whether the teenager is a boy or a girl. Girls most often choose narcotic overdose (mainly barbiturates, or sleeping pills), but boys do not demonstrate a single "favorite" method. One study showed that gas poisoning (especially carbon monoxide) was the most preferred method by both teenage boys and girls, but another study showed that teenage boys preferred firearms and hanging while teenage girls preferred poisoning (which includes drug overdose). Many studies show that adolescent boys tend to use a variety of active, fairly unique methods (such as decapitation, electrocution, or jumping under a school bus).

Poison (including drugs, such as sleeping pills) is the most frequent method of both attempted and successful suicide among adolescents.

If the adolescent is young or if the suicidal person is a child, there will be a difference in the method chosen for a simple reason: a child must choose a method that is both accessible and possible. The most common method among children is drugs and/or poisons — but the drugs must be available to the child, and the child must know something about the dangers of taking too many pills. A Swedish study encompassing a large number of child and adolescent suicides showed that the most common methods were the following, in order from most to least common:

1. Narcotic drugs (the overwhelming favorite)
2. Cutting
3. Hanging and strangulation
4. Poisoning with gas
5. Jumping from a height
6. Drowning (as many chose drowning as chose jumping)
7. Running in front of a moving vehicle
8. Swallowing a sharp object (tied with running in front of a vehicle
9. Shooting

A close look at the list shows that the choice of methods is logical. Most children have access to narcotic drugs — their parents' medicine chest usually has at least one or two prescription bottles full. Even a child can manage to take pills: it's easy, and most children have had practice with aspirin or antibiotics. On the other hand, few children have access to guns, know how to handle them, or know how to load ammunition into them.

How effective are the methods used by adolescents? Experts generally agree that the most lethal methods are as follows, in order from the most lethal to the least lethal:

1. Firearms and explosives (making a child's suicide less likely to succeed, since he rarely chooses a gun)
2. Jumping from a high place
3. Cutting vital organs
4. Hanging
5. Drowning, if the person does not know how to swim
6. Poison, both solid and liquid
7. Cutting of nonvital organs
8. Poisoning with gas (such as carbon monoxide, a favorite of many adolescents
9. Pain medications

If an adolescent chooses one of the more lethal methods — shooting himself or jumping from a high place, for example — his suicide is likely to be successful because death occurs quickly, leaving little chance for a rescue to take place. If an adolescent chooses a less lethal method, such as carbon monoxide poisoning or slashing the wrists, death occurs much more slowly, allowing plenty of time for intervention and rescue.

One disturbing trend that has recently drawn increasing attention is accidental suicide as a result of autoeroticism: almost always, these deaths involve a teenage boy who was hanging himself while masturbating. The boy cuts off just enough oxygen to the brain to experience extremely heightened response, and then loosens the noose before death occurs. In some cases, however, asphyxiation occurs before the boy can regain control, and the hanging death is mistakenly disgnosed as suicide.

Reluctance of parents and of the medical community to discuss autoerotic hanging deaths has contributed to the confusion and the mistaken claim of suicide. Some parents who discover their sons dress them, change their position, or do other things to mask the true cause of death. Apparently, many would rather cope with the stigma of suicide than admit to the boy's autoerotic activities. According to parents who *have* tried to seek information on the subject, public discussion is difficult to come by. One parent whose son died as a result of accidental asphyxiation during masturbation says she consulted physicians, mental health providers, psychiatrists, and officials at the private school her son attended; she says she was "treated with arrogance, viewed as a 'crazy,' and warned to stop discussing the subject, as any publicity would be dangerous to others who might imitate her son's sexual practices." She says that she was even stonewalled.

How Adolescent Suicide Differs From Adult Suicide

Other than choice of method, there are some factors that make adolescent suicide different from adult suicide. Syed Arshad Husain and Trish Vandiver, researchers from the

Department of Psychiatry at the University of Missouri-Columbia, have identified several ways in which adolescent suicide is distinctly different:

Distorted death concept/romanticized idea of death. As mentioned, the adolescent may not actually see suicide as a way of ending life or as a permanent, irreversible condition from which he can never return. He more often sees suicide (and the resulting death) as a comforting, gentle, nurturing, romanticized state that will somehow magically vanish, allowing life again at some point down the road. In sharp contrast, most adults who choose suicide intend that their lives should come to an abrupt end: they are choosing suicide as a form of relief or escape, but they are clearly aware of its permanence.

Suggestibility. Recent disturbing cases of cluster suicides illustrate clearly the degree of susceptibility that most adolescents have. A teenager who is feeling depressed or trapped may quickly opt for suicide if he sees someone else do it. Children and young adolescents are also susceptible to what researchers call a "psychic homicide," when a child who is the subject of hostility from parents actually feels the need to die.

Adults, on the other hand, vary widely in their susceptibility to suggestion. While some adults are highly suggestible, it is much less common than in children and adolescents.

Impulsiveness. Most adult suicides are controlled; most adolescent suicides are the result of an impulse. Adolescents are still at the stage of development when impulse control is weak; when confronted with frustration, depression, or anger, an adolescent may react on impulse with a suicide attempt. Fortunately, many impulsive suicide attempts are not successful: because they are done on impulse, they are poorly planned and allow for intervention or rescue. Interestingly, most adolescent impulse suicide attempts are not actual attempts to die — most often, they are attempts at revenge, retaliation, punishment, or getting attention. A teenager acting on impulse may slash his wrists in an effort to punish his parents for being such strict disciplinarians. His attempt at suicide is clearly an attempt to punish his parents, not an attempt to end his own life. He doesn't really see death as the final outcome — what he sees instead are his guilt-wracked parents suffering over the suicide attempt and changing their strict ways. He sees himself very much alive. If the suicide attempt backfires and is successful, it was likely due to accident rather than planning on the part of the teenager.

Turning aggression inward. Teenagers, as difficult as it is for them to admit, are still dependent on their parents or guardians — not only for physical needs but for many emotional needs as well. A teenager who begins to go through the normal development crisis of separating from her parents may begin to feel resentment, anger, hostility, or aggression toward them. But she is probably also incapable of expressing those feelings to her parents, so she turns them against herself instead. To her, it is unacceptable to hate her parents (on whom she is so dependent), but it is okay to hate herself. Sadly, suicide and

---

"When we are depressed, whatever our age, we need someone to listen to and understand our problems — someone who will see our world through our eyes. There is truth in the saying that 'A problem shared is a problem halved.' However, as every parent and friend knows, it is not always easy to initiate a conversation with a touchy or withdrawn youngster. One way to lead a teenager into sharing feelings is to share yours. When you say in effect, 'You seem to be feeling down and I know something about how that feels because I've been depressed,' you are telling the youngster that depression is normal, that even competent adults can feel it, that you respect his feelings and you care about him, that you want to listen to his problems."

—Youth Suicide National Center

death may be the price that some teenagers pay to gain domestic peace and acceptance.

This kind of reasoning is much less common in adult suicide.

Depression. As mentioned, depression is a leading cause of suicide among all age groups. The critical difference lies in the ability of parents to recognize and diagnose depression in an adolescent.

Depression in an adult is usually manifest in the "pure" state — the adult is tearful, sad, despondent, hopeless, and incapable of functioning as usual. Those same reactions may be demonstrated by a teenager — but a teenager may also react to depression by becoming bored, restless, defiant, angry, or delinquent. To an adult who is used to associating depression with sadness and feelings of worthlessness, a rebellious and bored teenager who starts running away from home, skipping school, or stealing money hardly fits the pattern. But these young people are often profoundly depressed, and their misery can sometimes rival that of an adult.

How You Can Help

If you suspect that a teenager you know is considering suicide, what can you do to help?

First of all, remember that *you can help*. Until death has occurred, it is never too late. All of the research done on suicide tells us that most suicidal people don't really want to die: they want to escape an intolerable situation, or they want to change their circumstances, or they want someone to reach out and care for them. Unfortunately, they see suicide as the only way of achieving their goals — they see no other alternatives.

You can provide those alternatives! You can take a person who is teetering on the edge between life and death, and you can push him toward life. Too many people think that a suicidal person is determined to die. That's simply not true — and you can help make him determined to live.

What Parents Can Do

The first and most important thing you can do to prevent teenage suicide — whether you are a parent, a teacher, a friend, or a counselor — is to never ignore a teenager's suicide threat. Whatever you do, take him seriously. Even if he is not actually planning on killing himself, his threat of suicide indicates that he is deeply troubled and in need of your help. Never, ever walk away thinking, "Oh, he's just going through one of those stages. He'll get over it. He doesn't really mean it." He probably *does* mean it — he might not mean that he wants to die, but he does mean that things for him are confusing, painful, and distressing. Wouldn't you rather err on the side of worrying too much about a possible suicide than walking away from a teenager who follows through?

If you are a parent, here are some of the things you can do to help prevent a suicide:

—If you notice some of the warning signs in your teenager, confront him or her. Don't ignore it, hoping it will go away or assuming your child is going through a phase. Sit down in an unemotional atmosphere and say, "I've been noticing that you seem kind of depressed lately. Is something bothering you?" If your child doesn't begin talking about his feelings, confront him more directly: "Do you ever wish you were dead?" If he says yes, ask, "Have you been thinking about killing yourself?"

"I tell young people to remember that suicide is a permanent answer to a temporary problem. And I tell parents to remember they are not *powerless when they sense their child is having trouble. There* are *things they can do, ranging from simply showing their concern and offering help in any way possible to going for professional help themselves, to actually forcing a child to go for help or hospitalization if necessary. And then whatever happens — because parents also have to remember that what a child does is ultimately his or her responsibility and, for reasons you will* never *understand, some people are going to take their own lives no matter what — you will know that you have done everything you could."*

—Iris Bolton, Director, The Link Counseling Center, Atlanta, Georgia

Don't worry — if he hasn't been thinking about it, your question won't plant the seeds in his mind. Your job is to get the problem out in the open. Your child is probably filled with despair, so it is up to you to take the initiative. Be aggressive: your child's life is at stake.

—**Watch for signs of depression, isolation, or distress.** If you determine that your child might be steering toward suicidal thoughts, take immediate action.

—**Listen to your teenager.** Really listen. Instead of concentrating on the words he is saying, try to understand what he is trying to say. Use the model of effective communication: First, listen with your full attention, and resist the urge to interrupt. Then repeat back to your child what you think he has said, using your own words. If you haven't gotten it right, he'll correct you. Remember that you might have to take the initiative, especially if you haven't been in the habit of communicating well with your child. If he hints at despair, you might have to be bold enough to say, "It sounds to me as though you are feeling real despair. When did you start feeling that way?"

—**Evaluate the seriousness of the situation, and carefully monitor the intensity of your child's emotions.** Your child is probably in a great deal of danger if she swings from being depressed to being restless and agitated.

—**Refrain from making judgments.** You are there to listen, not to pass judgment. You might think that your child is blowing things all out of proportion, and that being kicked off the baseball team is simply not reason enough to kill yourself over. That's *your* opinion. Your child may think it is an excellent reason. Try seeing things from his point of view You see his dismissal from the baseball team as one of those mildly irritating experiences in life that won't matter a bit two or three years down the road, and that will scarcely be remembered five or ten years down the road. He sees it as a major source of humiliation, embarrassment, and as a reflection on his own worthlessness; after all, if he was worth anything, the coach never would have kicked him off the team. Remember, too, that he doesn't have the ability to see five or ten years down the road: he is living in the here-and-now, and he has been devastated.

—Never react to your child with horror. You may never have entertained the thought of suicide, and the fact that your child is suicidal may be more than you can deal with. But remember — feelings of rejection probably led to your child's suicidal crisis to begin with. The last thing he needs is to feel like you are rejecting him again.

—Never deny your child's suicidal thoughts. Don't say, "Oh, you don't mean that. You don't really want to kill yourself." Your child has taken a big risk by telling you his feelings; he needs them validated, not put aside. However ridiculous they may seem to you, they are real to him. Acknowledge them; encourage your child to talk about his suicidal thoughts and to express his emotions. He may be more confused than anything else, and talking about it may help tremendously.

—Never try to use reverse psychology on a teenager who is contemplating suicide. Some parents, in an attempt to shock their children out of suicide, say something like, "Okay! Go ahead!" This is one situation in which reverse psychology doesn't work. Jess walked into his son Scott's bedroom just in time to discover Scott fingering the trigger of a handgun. Scott blurted out that he was distraught over losing his girlfriend, and that he was going to kill himself. Thinking that he could

"One fact is clear — parents should not dismiss the impact of an adolescent crisis that seems trivial by adult standards."

—Joyce Jurnovoy and David Jenness

trick his son out of it, Jess shouted, "Go ahead! Shoot!" In one fluid motion, Scott placed the butt of the revolver against his temple and pulled the trigger.

—Don't try to win any arguments about suicide. They simply can't be won. In your child's mind, there is no "right" side and "wrong" side. She's probably been considering this for some time, weighing out the alternatives in her mind and carefully sorting out the possibilities. She obviously sees suicide as a viable alternative (in fact, she probably sees it as the desirable alternative). She is convinced that she is right. Instead of trying to win an argument with her, concentrate on winning her trust and confidence.

—Help your teenager realize that what he is feeling is temporary and will pass. As discussed, adolescence brings on developmental changes that make this kind of farsighted vision impossible or difficult to attain. Don't try to lessen the severity of your child'd depression or agony; instead, identify with him, certify that his feelings are real, and then share some experience of your own that illustrates how you, too, felt bleak and depressed. After you have taken the time to show him that you know how he feels, make him realize that he will not always

"If we want to stop the suicide epidemic, we must break the conspiracy of silence that surrounds it. Cancer used to be something people kept as secret as possible — but because of campaigns to publicize and spread information about the disease, people learned to recognize symptoms and get early treatment that saved their lives. In the same way, early symptoms that may lead to young suicides can be publicized and taught. And if just one extra life can be saved because a friend has learned to help, that will be a beginning."

—Francine Klagsbrun, Too Young To Die: Youth and Suicide

feel that way. *Make him understand that he will start feeling better, no matter how bad things seem now, if he will give himself the time.*

—**Help your teenager realize that if he chooses to die, he is making a permanent decision that can never be reversed.** Help him understand that if he chooses some other way of coping with his problems — such as visiting the school counselor, going to the hospital, or moving to another town — he can always change his mind and try something else if the first solution doesn't work. If he commits suicide, though, he can never change his mind.

—**Allow your teenager to ventilate his feelings.** Don't be surprised if you discover a son or daughter you didn't know existed — a person who is hostile, angry, or despondent. He has probably been storing up his feelings for a long time, and they may come flooding out with intensity and explosiveness. Stay calm and listen without judging.

—**Remove all potential weapons of self-destruction from your home, even if you will be temporarily inconvenienced.** Arrange to have your guns locked in a safe-deposit box. Remove prescription drugs from the house, especially narcotics (such as sleeping pills). Get rid of razor blades and sharp knives. If you can, dismantle anything your son or daughter could hang him or herself from (such as a strong shower rod or closet rod). Let your child know what you are doing. Stress that you are not doing it because you distrust him, but because you desperately want him to stay alive.

—**Once you have determined that your child is suicidal, do not leave him alone, isolated, or unobserved for any appreciable length of time.** Until you can get help, stay with your child.

—**Be bold in expressing your emotions to your son or daughter.** Tell her how much you love her. Tell her how devastated you would be if she were dead. Tell her that you want more than anything for her to stay alive and to work out her problems. Tell her that you don't want her to be in pain, and that you want to help her make the pain go away without sacrificing her in the meantime. Your child may desperately need to hear that you love and care about her.

—Mobilize other family members into a life-support system for your teenager. Encourage them to tell the teenager how important he is to them, what a vital part of the family he is, and how much he would be missed if he were to leave.

—During your communication with your child, try to find out what has brought her to such a point of desperation. If you have anything to do with the cause, do what you can to correct it. If your child tells you that she feels too pressured to perform at school, back off; start stressing your child's strengths, such as her eye for beauty or her appreciation of good music, and stop pushing her to perform.

—Assure your child that no matter what happens, you will love him. If he fails his math class, if he loses the basketball game for the team, if he isn't able to get a date to the sophomore dance, so what? Those things don't matter to you. You will love him all the same. Stress the fact that you love your child for who he *is*, not what he *does*.

—Set guidelines and limits for your child. Jeane Westin, an author who has written several books about teenage suicide, says, "It's time for parents to trust themselves and use their own sources of strength to help their kids develop that strength, too. We mistakenly think that our children don't want to hear from us, that we're supposed to give them 'freedom' to express themselves without controls or restraints, but the truth is that they are desperate — sometimes even *dying* — to hear from us. They *want* guidelines and rules for their lives. We parents should be passing on to our children the best of our tradition, our wisdom, our strength."

—Encourage your child to do her best, but encourage her to take small steps to accomplish her goals.

—Stay involved in your teenager's life. Express an interest in what she is doing, how she is feeling, who her friends are, and what her problems are. Be there as an active, involved force.

—**If your child is having a suicidal crisis, give him something to hang on to.** Tell him you will get him help. Promise him that you will not desert him. Tell him that together you will find ways to solve the things that are bothering him.

—**Share your feelings with your child.** Charlotte Ross, executive director of the Youth Suicide National Center, suggests that sharing your own feelings and experiences with a depressed adolescent can help him share his. You might say something like, "You seem to be really depressed. I know what that is like, because I have felt depressed. I remember thinking that it would never end, would never go away. But it finally did end. I think some of the things I did helped," and so on.

—**Don't be afraid to get help.** You can only do so much on your own, and then professional help is needed. Charlotte Ross suggests emphasizing to your child that something is wrong in

"There are four things we've got to teach our kids in order to survive. We've got to develop an individual's self-esteem so that each person has an internalized, intrinsic value because of who he or she is, not because of what he or she does. We've got to teach communication skills so that each person can learn to express and discuss their feelings. And we've got to teach what I call 'positive failure.' In a culture that promotes being 'number one' in all we do, it's important for kids to know that the effort is positive, that they can enjoy and grow from what they do regardless of the outcome. And, finally, we've got to help individuals learn how to handle grief. Many suicides are triggered by some sort of a loss — a parent, a good grade, even a prom date — we've got to help people learn how to deal with losses and even grow from them."

—*Iris Bolton, The Link Counseling Center, Atlanta, Georgia*

his *life*, not that something is wrong with *him*. Your attitude can go a long way toward helping your child accept counseling. Never refer to professional counseling as something for the "crazy."

—Help your child realize that you intend to get to the bottom of the problem. Make it clear that you are *not* going to give up.

—Get help immediately. Take your child to a crisis intervention center, a suicide prevention clinic, or your local hospital. Be careful: you don't want to make him think that something is "wrong" with him. You might want to say something like, "I love you too much to see you take this drastic action, but I'm not sure what to do to help. I'm going to take you to the crisis intervention center, because there are people there who will know what to do. Together, we can work this out." Make it clear that you are not abandoning your child, deserting him, or "dumping him off" on somebody else. Make it clear that you will stay by his side until he gets his problems resolved.

—Don't be fooled if your child tells you that he was deeply distressed but he now feels better. He didn't get that way overnight, and he isn't going to feel better overnight. He may be

---

"People who believe they can accomplish something worthwhile are bound to feel good about themselves, which also holds for people who feel strong enough to overcome occasional failures. We show children we accept that they are valuable by expecting them to contribute and by having faith that they can manage things on their own. And nothing strengthens children's confidence in themselves more than when they discover they are capable of handling a difficult situation on their own and coming out the better for it."

—*Stanton Peele, author*, A Parent's Guide to Understanding and Preventing Drug and Alcohol Abuse

telling you he feels better so that you will leave him alone and let him have the privacy he needs to accomplish the suicide.

—**Don't expect instant improvement.** Patricia Couto, executive director of Nashville's Crisis Intervention Center, says, "There's virtually no way to convince a teenager that things aren't always going to be so bleak. As you get older you realize that. But with teens, no matter how you go about it, you have difficulty getting through because their pain is so intense." Appreciate the fact that your child is suffering greatly, and don't heap unrealistic expectations on her. Realize that the healing will take time and tremendous effort.

—**Teach appropriate values early.** Psychologist Stanton Peele, renowned for his work with adolescents in the prevention of drug and alcohol abuse, proposes a five-point system of teaching values to children. Dr. Peele's values that can help curb drug and alcohol abuse can also help stem the tide of teenage suicide — and they are values that need to be taught in the home by concerned, loving parents:

1.   *A sense of healthfulness and how to attain it.* A child who learns to value his physical and mental well-being is much less likely to

---

"It's time for parents to trust themselves and use their own sources of strength to help their kids develop that strength, too. We mistakenly think our children don't want to hear from us, that we're supposed to give them 'freedom' to express themselves without controls or restraints, but the truth is that they are desperate — sometimes even dying *— to hear from us. They* want *guidelines and rules for their lives. We parents should be passing on to our children the best of our tradition, our wisdom, our strength."*

—*Jeane Westin,* The Coming Parent Revolution: Why Parents Must Toss Out the Experts and Start Believing in Themselves Again

do things that will compromise his health and well-being — including, obviously, harming himself by committing suicide. There are plenty of things you can teach at home about how to maintain a strong, healthy body: the importance of good nutrition, for example, or how important it is to get plenty of sleep and regular exercise. Remember, too, that actions speak louder than words. It's up to you to set the pace in diet, exercise, rest, leisure, and prevention of illness.

2.　*A belief that it is worthwhile to get to the bottom of a problem.* As discussed, suicide is often a teenager's desperate attempt to solve a problem, not really a wish to die. Too many of our children lack problem-solving skills — and when presented with a difficult problem, they seek what they see as the only way "out."

Dr. Peele says, "Children learn to do for themselves, to endure discomfort, and to get to the bottom of a problem by being left to their own devices some of the time. They learn from such experiences how to surmount difficulties without someone constantly telling them what to do. They discover that just because something cannot be accomplished right away does not mean it can never be solved. And, most importantly, they find out that through the application of their own skills and efforts, they are likely to be able to handle just about anything that is thrown at them in life."

The message for parents?

"In coping with the task of establishing a sense of who and what one is and wants to become, the adolescent may become confused. The confusion may occur if the task is too difficult; if he or she has been forced to assume an incompatible role; or a formerly chosen role is inappropriate for current needs, values and views.

—*Youth Suicide National Center*

Don't solve your child's problems for him. Start early to encourage your child to use his own resources and to solve his own problems. It is those with the least tolerance and ability who fall victim to suicide.

3. *An appreciation of achievement and involvement in positive enterprise.* Help your children develop an appreciation for goals and hard work by letting them contribute to family life (and, therefore, letting them have accomplishments) even as tiny children. A three-year-old who is allowed to put placemats on the family dinner table each night swells with pride at his accomplishment; later, he'll want to capture that same feeling by doing other, more advanced things. An appreciation for achievement will help provide an alternative for plenty of the situations that can lead to teenage suicide.

There is an obvious word of caution here: step in. Get involved. Help your child set reasonable, realistic, attainable goals. His self-esteem will soar if he reaches a goal; it will be shattered if he doesn't. We're not saying that you should rush in and protect your child from disappointment. We *are* saying that you should not encourage your child to set himself up for disappointment!

4. *A sense of community and of obligation to others.* We've talked about the need to avoid social isolation and alienation; encouraging your child to get involved in the community from an early age can help prevent such isolation. Again, set the standard. Rear your child with the understanding that it is right to serve others; right to respect others; and right to seek out others.

5. *A sense of one's own value.* Perhaps your most important task is to help your child feel good about himself. Dr. Peele relates that researchers have discovered a healthy sense of self-esteem among children who are encouraged to get involved in the larger community. A child who has had experiences with accomplishment can begin to feel good about himself — and can find the strength he needs to cope with the times when he does not succeed. Nothing boosts self-esteem like the experience of being faced with a tough problem and solving it on your own!

What Teachers and Schools Can Do

—**Watch for signs of trouble in the adolescents you teach.** If you suspect that someone is in trouble, remain calm and nonjudgmental. Ask questions in a calm and straightforward way — something that will make clear to your student that you do care and that you want to make a difference.

—**You may need to come right out and ask the teenager if he is thinking about committing suicide.** Listen nonjudgmentally and encourage him to express his feelings. *Always take him seriously.*

—**Rely on your own judgment to determine how urgent the situation is.** Using the list of questions suggested earlier, try to figure out how high the risk is and act appropriately. If you determine that the teenager is a low risk for following through with the suicide, you may want to contact his parents within a day or two; if you determine that the risk is great, you may want to arrange to have him transported to a crisis intervention center, where you can phone his parents.

—**Involve the parents as soon as you can.** Be careful not to place blame or pass judgment. Be open and helpful, and work as

---

"Most young people who are self-destructive want someone to talk to about their feelings. They are confused and looking for someone to stop them. Schools can't offer long-term therapy, but they do have an obligation to help troubled kids. The purpose of our program is twofold: to create a public awareness of the problem and to provide an immediate support system for those who need it."

—*Thomas Barrett, School Psychologist and Initiator of The Cherry Creek Suicide Prevention Project, Denver*

a resource for the parents. Answer their questions with honesty and candor, and encourage them to talk to their son or daughter about what is going on.

—**Provide information for the parents on where they can go to get help.** If there isn't an established network in your school district, mobilize the counselor, other teachers, and other students.

—**Be affirmative but supportive with the teenager.** She is in a great deal of distress, and she needs strong, stable guides. Even if you are feeling panic-stricken and terrified by the potential suicide, give her the impression that you are calm and that you know what you are doing. Tell her you will do everything possible to get help for her to prevent her from taking her own life.

—**Do something tangible.** If one of your students has confessed feeling suicidal, don't make promises and then disappear into the sunset. Call the crisis intervention center in your community and make an appointment for your student to meet with a counselor. Ask your student's permission to call his parents, and then do it. Go with your student to the school counselor, and stay with him if he wants you to. Give him something to hang onto and something to look forward to — and whatever you do, don't desert him. If he feels that his confession was in vain, he will become even more despondent and frustrated.

—**If you think that your student is at a high risk for completing the suicide, don't leave him alone.** Arrange for someone to be with him until the worst of the crisis has passed. Call his parents, give him a ride home from school, or ask one or two other students to walk home with him and stay with him until an adult arrives with help. In a private setting, tell his parents that you suspect he is at high risk, and tell them why; encourage them to stay with him and get immediate help.

—**Encourage your student to talk to his parents and to express his feelings openly and honestly, even if it is painful.**

Offer to be with him while he talks to his parents; he may feel comforted and able to talk more openly with your support.

—**If a number of students in your classes seem to be going through a crisis, consider teaching a unit on teenage suicide.** Concentrate on teaching students that there are other ways of coping with problems, and work on banishing tunnel vision. You might work with the school counselor, the administration, and other teachers in developing a program in your school to deal with the problem of teenage suicide.

—**Be reluctant to keep a student's confidence when it comes to suicide.** Charlotte Ross and Russell Lee warn that fears and anxieties usually lie behind a student's need to keep his plans secret. A student may simply fear what others are going to think of him and his plan. Ross and Lee warn, too, that concern for a confidentiality must always take the back seat to concern for a student's life.

—**Resist the urge to offer "simple" solutions,** add Ross and Lee. Suicide and the pain that leads up to it are very complex problems — problems that can't be addressed with a shrug of the shoulders and an "Oh, well" attitude. Treat a suicide threat as the serious matter that it is. Make sure that your tone of voice, your physical gestures, and your verbal communication all tell the student that you are taking him seriously and that you want to do whatever you need to to prevent this death.

"The facts of death are as essential to the education of the young — and as intently sought — as the facts of life. In both instances, adolescents want to know about life and death because these subjects touch their deepest and most private feelings."

—*Charlotte P. Ross, Executive Director, Suicide Prevention and Crisis Center, San Mateo County, California, and President/Executive Director, Youth Suicide National Center*

—Resist the urge, too, to "take sides" with the adolescent against his family, warns St. Francis Xavier University Assistant Professor Angela Gillis. You might think you are doing him a favor, but think again: what he probably needs more than anything else is to be an integral part of his family and his peer group, not an entity separated from them with his teacher as an advocate. You may hear grim tales about the way a student is treated at home, but you should not choose up sides and go to war.

—Help your student identify the problems that have lead to the suicidal state, says Gillis. You may be surprised to find out that he doesn't really know what brought him to this point — or you may be just as surprised to hear a handful of "problems" at fault for the suicidal rage. Remember that the "problems" may sound trivial to you, but that they are all-inclusive to your student. He can't see beyond them; he can't understand that they will be solved and will no longer torture him.

Show him that his problems *can* be solved. After you identify them, one by one, help your student work out some solutions. Let him do most of the thinking, with your occasional guidance or suggestion. He needs to know that his problems *can* be solved and that he *can* cope with that solution process.

"In the beginning I did worry that all the attention paid to the subject might inadvertently get it going in terms of 'something to do.' But the cases we see don't indicate that this has happened. All in all, the press coverage has helped — it's much better to get this out in the open — and with the higher visibility comes a greater chance of mental health education. Because of these reports we can move in to reach more children — and we'll see more preventive measures."

—Dr. Mary Giffin, Medical Director, North Shore Mental Health Association, Northfield, Illinois

—**Remember that you should always check with your administrator to determine guidelines in referring a suicidal student to the proper professional authority.** Do not assume a treatment role yourself. Do not assume that you can "cure" a student on your own, without the assistance of a professional mental health worker.

Irving Berkovitz, the senior psychiatric consultant for schools for the Los Angeles Department of Mental Health, prescribes six steps that every school should take in preventing teenage suicide:

1.   Offer remedial reading classes; researchers have shown a strong correlation between poor reading skills and emotional distress.

2.   Help prevent withdrawal and social isolation by encouraging all students to participate in extracurricular activities and community service projects.

3. Include in the curriculum a more positive study of society, stressing problem-solving and the building of an interdependent world. Stress the need for responsibility and service to others to help children develop a sense of community.

4. Develop more positive and personalized teacher-student

"Education is our most valuable tool. I would like to see groups of experts go into school systems and talk to kids, parents, and teachers. I would also like to see schools set up programs not only on suicide prevention but on how to deal with stress and depression as well, since these are components of suicide and yet adolescents may not express them in the same way adults do."

—*Dr. Pamela Cantor, President, American Association of Suicidology*

relationships. If the classes in your school are too large, lobby with the principal and the school district to get class size reduced. Get involved with each student. Make sure that each student knows you care about him.

5. Try to see that each student has at least one friend.

6. See that the counselors in your school are allowed to counsel students — and that their time is not monopolized by administrative tasks. Executive assistants or secretaries can take care of most of the paperwork, filing, and assessment, freeing the counselors up to talk to students. Make sure that your counselors are fully educated about the problem of teenage suicide, and ask them to develop a specific plan for dealing with troubled students.

In essence, says Berkovitz, try to keep morale high among students and school personnel. Foster rich and rewarding relationships between teachers and students and between groups of students. Make sure that parents get involved, especially at the elementary school level. Build a strong curriculum that emphasizes community involvement and sense of self. And, above all, keep the school neat and attractive — a place where students want to be.

Testifying before the Ninety-Eighth Congress Subcommittee on Human Services, Iris Bolton, director of the Link Counseling Center in Atlanta, Georgia, suggested the following goals to help prevent youth suicide:

"Suicide attempts, successful or not, are almost never private. Not only are they communicative, but they are invariably intended to have some effect on survivors."

—*Victor M. Victoroff, M.D., Chief of Psychiatric Services, Cleveland's Huron Road Hospital*

---

1. To increase awareness of the problem of suicide among youth through education of students, teachers, counselors, principals, clergy, juvenile justice workers, mental health professionals, and families.

2. To educate as to predictors of the signs of suicide so as to prevent attempts and reduce the numbers of completed suicides.

3. To educate as to crisis intervention techniques.

4. To promote awareness of community and statewide resources including mental health centers, private and nonprofit agencies, poison control, tie-line, etc.

5. To educate as to the grief process following a suicide for friends, family, teachers, peers, clergy, etc. so as to support grieving individuals and minimize the stigma and frequent "contagion" effect of suicide.

6. To develop a program within the schools which deals with:
   a. Positive self-esteem
   b. Communication skills
   c. Relationships—getting in, maintaining, getting out appropriately
   d. Process of grief around loss
   e. Positive failure/positive success
   f. Life skills, i.e., decision-making, values clarification, problem-solving
   g. The meaning of life and death
   h. Avoiding loneliness and isolation by building support networks
   i. Stress management

7. To develop a training package to be replicated statewide to mobilize communities to preventive efforts against the incidence of suicide through:
   a. A trainer of trainer's manual
   b. Audiovisual aids

8. To conduct statewide workshops using manual and audiovisual aids to leave communities with resources of their own.

It is also essential that young people, parents, teachers, and other youth workers be made aware of the local treatment opportunities for youth who have feelings of sadness, hopelessness, helplessness, worthlessness, suicidal impulses, and other self-destructive tendencies. This requires careful coordination and support between school personnel and the various mental health professionals.

What Friends Can Do

If you think that a friend might be contemplating suicide, don't act as if nothing is wrong. The American Association of Suicidology stresses the importance of confronting the situation, drawing your friend out, and expressing your concern. Most people who feel suicidal don't really want to die at first; it's only when no one responds to their signals that they decide their only option is death.

—Ask your friend directly if he has been contemplating suicide. If he says he has, tell him how much you care about him and tell him you will do everything possible to keep him alive. Say something like, "You are one of the greatest friends I've ever had. I don't want to lose that."

—Act immediately to get help for your friend. Tell his parents, take him to your school counselor, go with him to the crisis intervention center or suicide prevention center, or get in touch with the suicide hotline at your school. Don't be afraid of causing a false alarm — be aggressive, and act quickly.

—Don't think that you have to provide all the answers. You can leave that to the professionals. Your role is to let your friend know that you care about her and that you want her to be alive.

—Encourage your friend to talk about his feelings, and be a willing listener. Some of the things you hear will be uncomfortable or difficult to handle; listen without making judgments, casting blame, or rejecting your friend. If you recognize some of the feelings, you might say something like, "I can relate. Last year when I wanted to get on the yearbook staff so badly, I was devastated when I didn't. I think I can appreciate how you are feeling now, and I remember how awful it was." Take as much time as is necessary. Be patient, too — your friend might repeat the same things over and over. Just remember what a relief it probably is to have someone to say it to.

—**Help your friend find out where she can go for help.** If there is a crisis center or hotline, put your friend in touch.

—**If your friend doesn't want to seek help or if your friend admits to having a specific suicide plan, you MUST get in touch with a responsible adult IMMEDIATELY.** Rose Wall, a crisis intervention counselor, says, "The person may say, 'Don't tell my parents,' but usually the person really *wants* someone to know." If your friend is at high risk, someone *needs* to know.

General Suggestions

—**Don't say, "I know how you feel" if you've never felt like killing yourself.** If you have never felt the kind of despair,

---

"The cardinal rule of suicide prevention is this: DO SOMETHING. If someone you know has attempted suicide and has not received professional care: GET HELP. If someone you know threatens to end his life: GET HELP. If someone you know has undergone a drastic change in his life and begins preparing wills or giving away personal possessions: GET HELP. Don't wait to see if other signs develop. Don't decide to consider it for awhile. Do it today. Tomorrow may be too late."

—*Jan Fawcett, M.D., Chairman, Department of Psychiatry,*
  Rush Medical College

discouragement, hopelessness, and sense of terrible isolation that prompts suicidal feelings, you truly *don't* know how it feels. Your offering will be shallow and meaningless.

—If you are the one who intervenes in a suicide attempt, be prepared for resistance. A person who has just failed in an attempt to kill himself will probably be extremely upset; he probably won't want you to "save" him. If he resists your efforts, immediately get help from other adults or call the police.

—Avoid the temptation to moralize. The last thing a suicidal teenager needs is to be told that she is stupid, wrong, shameful, or irresponsible. Your primary consideration should be to support and comfort the adolescent, not to pass judgment or analyze.

—Never promise anything that you can't deliver. You *can* promise that you will go with the teenager to the crisis intervention center, and that you will stay with him there; you *can't* promise him that he will feel better in the morning or that his depression will fade by the weekend.

—Don't try to handle the situation by yourself. Seek professional, adult help quickly.

—Communicate a message of hope. This is very different from promising that the teenager will feel better or will get over his problems immediately; instead, it is an attitude of optimism and faith that he has the resources and the strength and the

"The youngster needs reassurance, but is unlikely to confide in someone if experience has shown him that person is more likely to lecture than to understand."

—*Youth Suicide National Center*

stamina to pull through. You might say something like, "I know I can't fully appreciate how you feel right now. I do know what a great person you are, and I know that you have tackled plenty of difficult problems in your life. I have to believe in you now, even though the odds seem stacked against you."

In summary, take the time. Get involved. Know that it will be difficult — maybe the hardest thing you've ever done in your life — but that you may be instrumental in saving a person's life. One student who came through her own suicidal crisis sums up what it is all about: "When one of my friends who was a little younger committed suicide, my first reaction was, 'Why didn't you *wait* another year?' I saw so many kids going through what I went through — for awhile *I'd* been so depressed I thought about killing myself, too — and I wish they could have known things would be better if they just waited it out. I know of someone who killed herself when she was fourteen. Fourteen! You haven't begun to know the most meaningful things in the world yet!"

Psychological First Aid

In summary, Dr. Calvin J. Frederick suggests the following preventive steps for the mature adult dealing with a suicidal youngster:

"When in doubt, it is always better to seek advice or to approach the subject directly than to wait and hope it will all 'go away.' It may — but it may not, and a youngster's life is too important to risk."

—Youth Suicide National Center

Step 1: Listen.

The first thing a person in a mental crisis needs is someone who will listen and really hear what he is saying. Every effort should be made to understand the feelings behind the words.

Step 2: Evaluate the seriousness of the person's thoughts and feelings.

If the person has made clear self-destructive plans, however, the problem is apt to be more acute than when his thinking is less definite.

Step 3: Evaluate the intensity or severity of the emotional disturbance.

It is possible that the person may be extremely upset but not suicidal. If a person has been depressed and then becomes agitated and moves about restlessly, it is usually cause for alarm.

Step 4: Take every complaint and feeling the person expresses seriously.

Do not dismiss or undervalue what the person is saying. In some instances, the person may express his difficulty in a low key, but beneath his seeming calm may be profoundly distressed feelings. *All* suicidal talk should be taken seriously.

Step 5: Do not be afraid to ask directly if the individual has entertained thoughts of suicide.

Suicide may be suggested but not openly mentioned in the crisis period. Experience shows that harm is rarely done by inquiring directly into such thoughts at an appropriate time. As a matter of fact, the individual frequently welcomes the query and is glad to have the opportunity to open up and bring it out.

Step 6: Do not be misled by the person's comment that he is past his emotional crisis.

Often the teenager will feel initial relief after talking of suicide, but the same thinking will recur later. Follow-up is crucial to insure a treatment effort.

Step 7: Be affirmative but supportive.

Strong, stable guideposts are essential in the life of a distressed individual. Provide emotional strength by giving the impression that you know what you are doing and that everything possible will be done to prevent the young person from taking his life.

Step 8: Evaluate the resources available.

The individual may have both inner psychological resources, including various mechanisms for rationalization and intellectualization which can be strengthened and supported, and outer resources in the environment, such as ministers, relatives, and friends whom one can contact. If these are absent, the problem is much more serious. Continuing observation and support are vital.

Step 9: Act specifically.

Do something tangible; that is, give the youngster something definite to hang onto, such as arranging to see him later or subsequently contacting another person. Nothing is more frustrating to the person than to feel as though he has received nothing from the meeting.

Step 10: Do not avoid asking for assistance and consultation.

Call upon whomever is needed, depending upon the severity of the case. Do not try to handle everything alone. Convey an attitude of firmness and composure to the person so that he will feel something realistic and appropriate is being done to help him.

Additional preventive techniques for dealing with persons in a suicide crisis may require the following:

—Arrange for a receptive individual to stay with the youth during the acute crisis.

—Do not treat the teenager with horror or deny his thinking.

—Make the environment as safe and provocation-free as possible.

—Never challenge the individual in an attempt to shock him out of his ideas.

—Do not try to win arguments about suicide; they cannot be won.

—Offer and supply emotional support for life.

—Give reassurance that depressed feelings are temporary and will pass.

—Mention that if the choice is to die, the decision can never be reversed.

How To Identify and Prevent Adolescent Suicide

Most suicide studies to date have been based on adults, and therefore their list of predictors (broken home, police contact, presence of psychosis, lethality of prior attempt) are of questionable use for adolescents. For instance, serious overt depression has been consistently related to suicide, but because depression in adolescent populations is extremely high anyway, it cannot be used as a predictor.

Other predictors are more applicable to adolescents: for instance, up to 78 percent of suicide attempts by adolescents have been found to have been precipitated by family fights and 30 percent of adolescent runaways have been found to have attempted suicide. Still, family fights and runaway attempts are so common that they too are of dubious value for prediction purposes.

Mary Jane Rotheram of the Columbia University College of Physicians and Surgeons Department of Child Psychiatry, has devised a simple clinical procedure which she says can evaluate whether an adolescent is in imminent danger to him- or herself, she reported at the recent Orthopsychiatric Association convention. It begins with a brief, 10-minute interview which tries to find evidence of current suicide ideation. Evidence of five of the following factors is enough to indicate suicide potential: gender is male, a past attempt with a method other than ingestion, more than one previous attempt, a history of anti-social behavior, having a close friend who committed suicide or a family member who attempted suicide, frequent drug and alcohol use, depression and dissimilarity between the youth and his or her environment.

A second interview of 20 to 30 minutes attempts to take preventive actions by the following four tasks:

1. A written promise is requested stating that the youth will not engage in suicidal behavior for a specified period, say, for two weeks.

2. The evaluator attempts to counteract negativism by supporting strengths and delivering compliments, and requests the adolescent to give self-rewards.

3. Although adolescent suicides frequently follow family arguments, the adolescents typically report that they did not feel consciously upset at the time of the attempt. Therefore they are taught to construct a "Feeling Thermometer" with a scale from 0-100 for most upset. The youth imagines 10 situations with varying degrees of discomfort, with the top of the scale describing situations which are likely to be suicide-eliciting. "For one youth, it may be being beaten by his/her father," Rotheram told Ortho. For another, it may be being homeless with no idea of where to go for the night, for a third, it may be a grade of 'B' on a math test. Being able to construct such a hierarchy indicates an ability to differentiate emotional states and suggests to the evaluator that the youth will be aware of feelings mounting in intensity.

4. Having constructed a Feeling Thermometer, the youths are asked to plan (and write down if necessary) how to handle themselves in a situation of 100. For example, a youth who becomes suicidal when her heroin-addicted father presents himself at the family home, wrote her plan on a file card which she carries with her constantly, saying she can (a) tell him to go away without opening the door, (b) climb out the window to a neighbor's house, (c) call out the window to someone on the street to call the police, or (d) pretend she is not home.

Rotheram feels this evaluation and action program can be taught to those most likely to contact suicidal youths, i.e., teachers, child care workers, nurses, and psychologists. It screens better than other scales and provides immediate action to prevent danger to the self short of hospitalization.

—*Reprinted with permission from* Behavior Today Newsletter, *May 5, 1986, pp. 6-7, 2315 Broadway, New York, NY 10024*

Bibliography

Abercrombie, Roland K. "A Compassionate Solution." *American Journal of Nursing*, May 1984, p. 597.

"Accidents Mask Kids' Suicides." *Medical World News*, June 13, 1983, p. 56.

Adolescence and Depression. U.S. Department of Health and Human Services, National Institute of Mental Health, Rockville, Maryland (ADM) 84-13337, 1984.

Alder, Jerry, and Shawn Doherty. "Kids: The Deadliest Game?" *Newsweek*, September 9, 1985, p. 93.

Allinson-Tomlinson, Minnie. "Adolescent Suicide." *Continuing Education*, September 1981, pp. 33-35.

Alper, Joseph. "Depression At An Early Age." *Science 86*, May 1986.

Altschul, Sol. "Children's Adjustment to a Parent's Death." *Physician & Patient*, January 1984, pp. 64-68, 70.

American Academy of Child Psychiatry and the National Council of Community Mental Health Centers. "Teenagers Are Focus of Mental Health Month." *Behavior Today Newsletter*, April 21, 1986.

American Association of Suicidology. *Suicide and Life-Threatening Behavior*, Vol. 11, No. 2. New York: Human Sciences Press, Inc., 1981.

American Association of Suicidology. *Suicide and Life-Threatening Behavior*, Vol. 11, No. 3. New York: Human Sciences Press, Inc., 1981.

"APA Panel Splits Over Rationality of Suicide in Specific Circumstances." *Medical World News*, June 11, 1984, pp. 11-12.

Baechler, Jean. *Suicides, Suicides, Suicides, Suicides, Suicides*. New York: Basic Books, Inc., Publishers, 1975.

Bassuk, Ellen L. "The Prevention of Suicide: Is It Possible?" *Emergency Decisions*, March 1985, pp. 24-33.

Battin, Margaret P. *Ethical Issues in Suicide*. New Jersey: Prentice-Hall, Inc., 1982.

Battin, Margaret P., and Ronald W. Maris. *Suicide and Life-Threatening Behavior: Suicide and Ethics*, Vol. 13, No. 4. New York: Human Sciences Press, Inc., 1983.

Beck, Aaron T., Harvey L.P. Resnick, Dan J. Lettieri. *The Prediction of Suicide*. Maryland: The Charles Press Publishers, Inc., 1974.

Berg, Donald E. "A Plan for Preventing Student Suicide." *Mental Health and the Schools. American Journal of School Health*. January 1973, pp. 126-140.

"Behind the Explosion in Self-Help Groups." *U.S. News & World Report*, May 2, 1983, p. 33.

Berman, Alan L. "The Teenager at Risk for Suicide." *Medical Aspects of Human Sexuality*, May 1985, pp. 123-130.

Blake, Patricia. "Going Gentle into that Good Night." *Time*, March 21, 1983, p. 85.

Bollet, Alfred J. "On Helping People Commit Suicide." *Medical Times*, March 1985, pp. 23-24.

Bruni, Patricia J. "Study Links Teen Suicide and Birth Factors." *Patient Care*, June 30, 1985, pp. 17-18.

Burns, David D. "The Perfectionists Script for Self-Defeat." *Psychology Today*, November 1980, pp. 34-52.

Carmack, Betty J. "Suspect a Suicide?" *RN*, April 1983, pp. 43-45, 90.

Check, William A. "Homicide, Suicide, Other Violence Gain Increasing Medical Attention." *Medical News*, August 9, 1985, pp. 721-723.

"Childhood Depression: New-and-Old-ways to Spot It." *Medical World News*, March 1, 1982, pp. 90-92.

Cole, William. "Early Warning Signals of Teenage Suicide." *Better Homes and Gardens*, October 1985, p. 22.

Colt, George H. "Suicide." *Harvard Magazine*, September-October 1983, pp. 47-66.

Corder, Billie F. "Recognizing Suicidal Behavior in Children." *Medical Times*, September 1982, pp. 25s-30s.

Davis, Patricia A. *Suicidal Adolescents*. Springfield: Charles C. Thomas, 1983.

"Death by Imitation? Experts Disagree on Issue of Teen 'Suicide Contagion.' " *Medical World News*, April 9, 1984, pp. 45-46.

Doan, Michael, and Sarah Peterson. "As 'Cluster Suicides' Take Toll of Teenagers—." *U.S. News & World Report*, November 12, 1984, pp. 49-50.

Elkind, David. "How Are Childen Affected by Divorce?" *Physician & Patient*, March 1985, pp. 10-15, 51.

Evans, David L. "Explaining Suicide Among the Young: An Analytical Review of the Literature." *HPNMHS*, August 1982, pp. 9-15.

Everstine, Dians S., and Louis Everstine. *People in Crisis: Strategic Therapeutic Interventions*. New York: Brunner/Mazel, 1983.

Everstine, Diane S., and Louis Everstine. *People in Crisis: Strategic Therapeutic Interventions*. New York: Brunner/Mazel, 1983.

Farberow, Norman L. *The Many Faces of Suicide: Indirect Self-Destructive Behavior*. McGraw-Hill Book Company, 1980.

Feinstein, Sherman C., John G. Looney, Allan Z. Schqartzberg, and Arthur D. Sorosky. *Adolescent Psychiatry: Volume IX—Developmental and Clinical Studies*. Chicago: The University of Chicago Press, 1981.

"15% of Teens Between 16 and 19 Estranged and Unlikely to Become Productive Adults." *Deseret News*, November 2, 1985, pp. A1-A2.

Fleming, Thomas C. "Suicide, the Hush-Hush Killer." *Postgraduate Medicine*, December 1981, pp. 13, 16.

Franklin, Neshama. "Dealing with the Blues and Depression." *Medical Self Care*, Spring 1982, pp. 10, 12, 14-16.

Frederick, Calvin J. "Self-Destructive Behavior Among Adolescents." *Mental Health and the Schools*, National Institute of Mental Health, pp. 119-125.

Gelman, David, and B.K. Gangelhoff. "Teen-age Suicide in the Sun Belt." *Newsweek*, August 15, 1983, pp. 70-74.

Gernsbacher, Larry M. *The Suicide Syndrome*. New York: Human Sciences Press, 1985.

Gillis, Angela. "Early Detection of the Suicidal Adolescent." *Psychiatry Nursing*, October/November/December 1984, pp. 6-8.

"Groups that Help You Through Hard Times." *Good Housekeeping*, October 1983, p. 267.

Hafen, Brent Q., and Brenda Peterson. "Preventing Adolescent Suicide." *Nursing*, October 1983, pp. 47-48.

Hafen, Brent Q., and Kathryn J. Frandsen. *Faces of Death: Grief, Dying, Euthanasia, Suicide*. Denver: Morton Publishing Company, 1983.

Hafen, Brent Q., and Kathryn J. Frandsen. *Psychological Emergencies & Crisis Intervention*. Denver: Morton Publishing Company, 1985.

Hals, Elaine. "Suicide Prevention." *Health Education*, August/September 1985, pp. 1, 45-47.

Hatton, Corrinne L., Sharon M. Valente, and Alice Rink. *Suicide: Assessment & Intervention*. New York: Appleton-Century-Crofts, 1977.

Hawkins, Steve L. "Rat Pack Youth: Teenage Rebels in Suburbia." *U.S. News & World Report*, March 11, 1985, pp. 51-54.

"Hemlock Society Will Tell How to Commit Suicide." *Medical World*

News, September 15, 1980, pp. 28-29.

Hendin, Herbert. *Suicide in America*. New York: W.W. Norton & Company, 1982.

Hendry, George S. "Possible Reasons for Teen-Age Suicide." *Physician & Patient*, January 1985, pp. 23-24, 30-32.

Herth, Kaye. "Loneliness." *The Journal of Practical Nursing*, November/December 1983, pp. 16-18.

"High Teenage Mortality Blamed on Life-Styles." *Medical World News*, October 24, 1983, p. 60.

Hoff, LeeAnn, and Marcia Resing. "Was This Suicide Preventable?" *American Journal of Nursing*, July 1982, pp. 1107-1111.

"How Can Parents Advise Children about Coping with Violence?" *Medical Aspects of Human Sexuality*, February 1984, pp. 104, 109-110, 115.

"How Death Haunts the Living." *U.S. News & World Report*, June 20, 1983, p. 67.

Human Potential, October 1985.

Hunter, Knoxice, Jack O. Jenkins, and Leonard A. Hampton. "Suicide: An EMS Primer." *Emergency*, July 1982, pp. 45-47.

Hurley, Dan. "Arresting Delinquency." *Psychology Today*, March 1985, pp. 58-61.

Husain, Syed Arshad, and Trish Vandiver. *Suicide in Children and Adolescents*. New York: Spectrum Publications, Inc., 1984.

"Indian Suicides Rising." *Children Today*, July/August 1984, p. 4.

Joan, Polly. *Preventing Teenage Suicide*. New York: Human Sciences Press, Inc., 1986.

Jurnovoy, Joyce, and Dennis Jenness. "Teenage Suicide." *Good Housekeeping*, pp. 86, 89-90, 92, 94.

Jurnovoy, Joyce, and Dennis Jenness. "The Tragic Impulse: Teenage

Suicide." *America's Health*, Vol. 6, No. 3, 1984, pp. 4-5.

J.W.M. "Childhood Depression: The Hidden Disease." *Good Housekeeping*, April 1984, p. 300.

Kim, Wun J. "Teenage Depression." *Medical Aspects of Human Sexuality*, January 1985, pp. 161-168.

Klagsbrun, Francine. "Preventing Teenage Suicide." *Family Health/Today's Health*, April 1977, pp. 21-24.

Lagone, John. "Too Weary to Go On." *Discover*, November 1981, pp. 72, 74, 76.

Levine, Saul. "Helping Young People Leave Cults." *Physician & Patient*, September/October 1985, pp. 45-51.

Levine, Saul. "Why Middle-Class Young People Join Cults." *Physician & Patient*, July/August 1985, pp. 18-22.

Linzer, Norman. *Suicide: The Will to Live vs. The Will to Die*. New York: Human Sciences Press, Inc., 1984.

McDermott, John F. "Childhood Depression." *Consultant*, April 1982, pp. 230, 237-239, 242-243, 246, 248-249

Mackey, Aurora. "The Frightening Facts about Teen Suicide." *Teen*, October 1983, pp. 10, 12, 93-94.

Maloney, Lawrence. "Suicide and Mercy Killing." *U.S. News & World Report*, July 11, 1983, pp. 63-65.

Maris, Ronald. "The Adolescent Suicide Problem." *Suicide and Life Threatening Behavior*, Vol. 15, No. 2, Summer 1985, p. 109.

Mead, Cheryl. "Why Teenagers are Killing Themselves." *Co-Ed*, September 1984, pp. 67-68, 70-72.

Mednick, Sarnoff. "Crime in the Family Tree." *Psychology Today*, March 1985, pp. 58-61.

Miles, Dwight. "Blacks Are At High Risk for Suicide." *Behavior Today Newsletter*, March 17, 1986, p. 2.

Motto, Jerome A. "Assessment of Suicide Risk." *Medical Aspects of Human Sexuality*, October 1984, pp. 134, 138-139, 142, 147-148, 153.

Murphy, George E. "On Suicide Prediction and Prevention." *Arch. Gen. Psychiatry*, March 1983, pp. 343-344.

National Institute on Drug Abuse. *Adolescent Peer Pressure: Theory, Correlates, and Program Implications.* Maryland: U.S. Department of Human Services, 1981.

Neely, Keith. "The Holiday Depression Syndrome." *JEMS*, December 1983, pp. 50-51.

O'Roark, Mary Ann. "The Alarming Rise in Teenage Suicide." *McCall's*, January 1982, pp. 14-15, 22, 120.

Osgood, Nancy J. "Suicide in the Elderly: Are We Heeding the Warnings?" *Postgraduate Medicine*, Auguat 1982, pp. 123-126, 128, 130.

"Parents of Sons Hanged During Auto-Erotic Activity Speak Out." *Sexuality Today*, May 20, 1985, pp. 1-2.

Patterson, William M., Henry H. Dohn, Julian Bird, and Gary A. Patterson. "Evaluation of Suicidal Patients: The SAD PERSONS Scale." *Psychosomatics*, April 1983, pp. 343-345, 348-349.

Peck, Michael L., Norman L. Farberow, and Robert E. Litman. *Youth Suicide.* New York: Springer Publishing, 1985, pp. 1-19.

Peele, Stanton. "Influencing Children's Use of Drugs—The Family's Role in Values Communication." *Focus on Family Magazine*, September/October 1984, p. 5.

Pfeffer, Cynthia R. *The Suicidal Child.* New York: The Guilford Press, 1986.

Pfeffer, Cynthia R., interview, "Suicidal Tendencies in Children and Adolescents," *Medical Aspects of Human Sexuality*, February 1986, p. 67.

Pietropinto, Anthony. "Effects of Unhappy Marriages on Children." *Medical Aspects of Human Sexuality*, February 1985, pp. 173-176, 181.

Pietropinto, Anthony. "Loneliness." *Medical Aspects of Human Sexuality*,

February 1985, pp. 241-143, 247-248, 251-252.

Pines, Maya. "Suicide Signals." *Science 83*, October 1983, pp. 55-58.

Praeger, Susan G., and G.R. Bernhardt. "Survivors of Suicide: A Community in Need." *Family & Community Health*, November 1985, pp. 62-72.

Rawlings, Gary, and Philip Hoile. "Handling the Suicide Call." *JEMS*, June 1982, pp. 140-142.

"Recognizing and Helping Others Who May be Suicidal." *The Medical Forum*, October 1981, pp. 3-4.

Renshaw, Domenna C. "Suicide in Children." *AFP*, December 1981, pp. 123-127.

Rogers, J., A. Sheldon, C. Barwick, K. Letofsky, and W. Lancee. "Help for Families of Suicide: Survivors Support Program." *Canadian Journal of Psychiatry*, October 1982, pp. 444-448.

Rosenthal, Perihana, and Stuart Rosenthal. "Suicide Among Preschoolers: Fact or Fallacy?" *Children Today*, November/December 1983, pp. 22-24.

Ross, Charlotte P. "Mobilizing Schools for Suicide Prevention." *Suicide and Life-Threatening Behavior*, Winter 1980, pp. 239-243.

Ross, Charlotte P. *Youth Suicide and What You Can Do About It.* October 30, 1984.

Rotheram, Mary Jane. "How To Identify and Prevent Adolescent Suicide." *Behavior Today Newsletter*, May 5, 1986, pp. 6-7.

Russakoff, L. Mark. "Suicide Warnings." *Physician & Patient*, August 1984, p. 35.

Shneidman, Edwin. *Definition of Suicide.* New York: John Wiley & Sons, Inc., 1985.

Silber, Tomas J. "Functional Disorders during Adolescence." *Medical Aspects of Human Sexuality*, September 1985, pp. 42-43, 46-47, 51-52, 56-57.

"Some Toddlers' 'Accidents' May Be Suicide Tries, Psychiatrist Reports." *Medical World News,* July 19, 1982, pp. 34-35.

Spoonhour, Anne. "Teen Suicide: The First Few Days are the Hardest." *Lookout,* pp. 76-78, 83-89.

"Statement from the American Academy of Child Psychiatry." *Physician & Patient,* January 1985, p. 30.

Stone, Elizabeth. "An Optimist Writes about Suicide, Confinement, and Despair." *Ms,* July 1983, pp. 55, 57-59.

Sudak, Howard S., et. al. *Suicide in the Young.* Boston: John Wright-PSG, Inc., 1984.

"Suicide in Adolescents." *Medical Aspects of Human Sexuality,* June 1985, pp. 159-160, 165, 168-170.

"Suicide in America." *Medical Essay,* September 1985, pp. 1-8.

"Suicide No. 2 Cause of Teen Deaths in the United States." *The Daily Herald,* May 16, 1984, p. 21.

"Suicide Touches Off Fear of Epidemic." *The Daily Herald,* March 21, 1985.

"The Adolescent in Despair." *Emergency Medicine,* September 30, 1985, pp. 51-54, 60, 63-66.

Thornton, Jeannye. "Behind a Surge in Suicides of Young People." *U.S. News & World Report,* June 20, 1983, p. 66.

Time Magazine, "Could Suicide Be Contagious," February 24, 1986, p. 59.

Tishler, Carl L., and Patrick C. McKenry. "Intrapsychic Symptom Dimensions of Adolescent Suicide Attempts." *The Journal of Family Practice,* Vol. 16, No. 4, 1983, pp. 731-734.

"Unraveling the Tragic Threads of Youth Suicide." *Medical World News,* July 22, 1985, pp. 123-130.

U.S. Committee on the Judiciary, U.S. Senate. "Oversight on the Factors that May Lead to Teenage Suicide and What May Be Done

To Prevent That Tragedy," October 3, 1984, Serial No. J-98-143.

U.S. Congress. "Suicide and Suicide Prevention: A Briefing by the Subcommittee on Human Services of the Select Committee on Aging," 1985. 98th Congress, 2d sess., Comm. Pub. No. 98-497.

U.S. Department of Health and Human Services. *Adolescent and Depression.*

U.S. Department of Health and Human Services. "Suicide Prevention: The Challenge for Nurses." U.S. Department of Health and Human Services, August 1981, pp. 5-28.

Valente, Sharon. "The Suicidal Teenager." *Nursing 85*, December 1985, pp. 47-49.

VanOrman, William, and John B. Murdock. *Crisis Counseling with Children and Adolescents.* New York: Continuum Publishing Company, 1983.

Victoroff, Victor. "Who Could Have Predicted Suicide?" *Diagnosis*, January 1982, pp. 63, 66-67, 71.

Warner, Carmen G. *Conflict Intervention in Social and Domestic Violence.* Maryland: Robert J. Brady Co., 1981.

Waters, Harry F. " Taking on Teen Suicide." *Newsweek*, October 29, 1984, p. 114.

Weinstein, Kate. "The Restless Mind: Boredom—America's Number One Health Hazard?" *Feeling Great*, pp. 64-67.

Weiss, Michael J. "The Riddle of Teenage Suicide." *ladies' Home Journal*, June 1984, pp. 54, 56-57, 167, 171-172.

Wells, Carl F., and Irving R. Stuart. *Self-Destructive Behavior in Children and Adolescents.* New York: Van Nostrand Reinhold Company, 1981.

"When a Teenager Gets Really Depressed." *Changing Times*, June 1982, pp. 27-28.

Whitworth, Russel A. "The Ethics of Suicide Intervention: Seen as a Nursing Problem." *Psychiatric Nursing*, January/February/March 1982, pp. 12-14.

"Why 30,000 Americans Will Commit Suicide This Year." *U.S. News & World Report*, April 1, 1984, pp. 48, 50.

"Wind River's Lost Generation." *Time*, October 21, 1985, p. 40.

Index

ORDER FORM

To order additional copies of **Youth Suicide: Depression and Loneliness**, fill in the following information and send it, along with a check or Mastercard/Visa information, to Cordillera Press, Inc., P.O. Box 3699, Evergreen, Colorado 80439. You may also phone in your credit card orders to (303) 670-3010.

□ Check Enclosed   □ Mastercard   □ Visa

Please send me ___ copies of **Youth Suicide: Depression and Loneliness** at $9.95 each. Add $1.00 postage per copy.
(Colorado residents add 3% sales tax)

Name: _____

Address: _____

City, State, Zip _____

Card Number: _____

Expiration Date: _____

Signature: _____

Note: Wholesale rates are available for qualified organizations and distributors on orders of more than 10 books. Please query the Publisher.